REBEL

REBEL

_____

THE RADICAL TEACHINGS OF JESUS

GREG HAUGH

BARTON HILL BOOKS

Printed in the United States of America

Edited by Andrew Kroeger and Elijah Dove

Published by Barton Hill Books

www.bartonhillbooks.com

ISBN: 978-0-9996372-2-7

CONTENTS

This book is dedicated to my dad, Terry Haugh, who passed away a few months ago. I love you forever and look forward to seeing you soon. Please say hi to Grandma, Grandpa, and Jono.

INTRODUCTION

If we are brutally honest, I bet the reason most of us are pretty bored and uninterested in Jesus is because we tend to think of him as a combination of Mr. Rogers and Santa Claus. Like Mr. Rogers, we mistakenly think that all Jesus did was be really nice and kind to everyone, and we incorrectly assume his message was basically to try to make people nice as well.

Because of this, we also mistakenly assume that being a Christian, or following Jesus, is all about trying to become a nicer version of what we are right now.

Or, like Santa Claus, we think of Jesus as sort of a jolly ol' chap who is keeping a list of the things we do right and wrong, and that he will ultimately pay us back for those deeds someday. I understand why so many people mistakenly think about Jesus like that, because I used to do this as well. I didn't come to faith until I was in my 20's, and until then, I assumed Jesus was like a combination of these two fictitious people, Mr. Rogers and Santa Claus.

If that's the way many of us think about Jesus, then it's no wonder it's almost impossible for us to take him seriously. No wonder it's almost impossible for some of us to commit our lives to following him.

After all, if our ideas about Jesus are based on a Christmas character that exists only in fantasies, or a T.V. character who is so amazingly kind and nice that none of us can relate to him, then of course we won't be able to take Jesus seriously or relate to him in any meaningful way.

Of course his words and teachings will seem completely boring, distant, and disconnected from the painful issues we often face in the real world. But if we can somehow put away these inaccurate concepts and ideas, and instead take him as seriously as we would take any other historical figure, then I am convinced he will change us and we'll never be the same again.

I am convinced that if we can do that, we will be in awe of just how dangerous, radical, revolutionary, controversial, subversive, and counter-cultural the real Jesus is. After all, Jesus was executed, and no one is executed for being nice. No one would ever try to execute Mr. Rogers, because he was so hopelessly nice that he would never do anything to anger anyone.

But Jesus did.

In this book, we are going to study the most radical teachings of Jesus so we can discover just how revolutionary he was and begin to take him as seriously as we do any other historical figure.

My hope is that we will respond by committing our lives to follow him.

My hope is that we will awaken from our boring and small ideas about Jesus.

My hope is that we will be inspired by the most dangerous revolutionary who has ever set foot on the earth.

My hope is that none of us will ever be the same again.

Welcome to the journey.

I

THE UNLIKELY MESSIAH

1

JESUS AS SAVIOR

The reason the concept of the unlikely messiah is so radical is because from day one of his ministry, Jesus had to challenge and fight against all kinds of incorrect assumptions and beliefs about who the messiah was supposed to be. The Jews of his day all thought the messiah would lead a physical war of violence, destruction, and death, so Jesus constantly had to explain what kind of messiah and king he really was. He had to shatter their expectations about him, and that's why this concept is so important and revolutionary.

The Kingdom of God Is Near, Repent and Believe

At the beginning of all four Gospels, there is a saying from Jesus about being sent to proclaim the good news (the Gospel) that the kingdom of God was near or at hand. [1] This is a radical and loaded phrase that we need to unpack to comprehend, but, before we do, here is the account from Mark's Gospel:

Now after John was arrested, Jesus came to Galilee, proclaiming the
good news of God, and saying, "The time is fulfilled, and the kingdom
of God has come near; repent, and believe in the good news." [2]

To understand how revolutionary the phrase *the kingdom of God* was back then, we need to take a short trip through ancient Jewish history. The Jews had been enslaved by the Egyptians for 400 years, but eventually God freed them from their slavery in Egypt. Then, about 1,000 years before Jesus walked the earth, God set them up in their own land, and gave them a united nation of Israel that lasted for three kings: King Saul, King David, and King Solomon.

But, immediately after the reigns of these three kings, the single united nation of Israel divided into two nations: the northern kingdom and the southern kingdom.

The kings and people of the northern kingdom were corrupt and evil. God sent prophet after prophet to call them to repent and turn back to God's ways, but they refused. Finally, without any other choice, God said he was going to destroy them if they didn't listen and change, but they continued to rebel.

So God called the nation of Assyria to make war against the northern kingdom of Israel and destroy it; and they did. The northern kingdom was destroyed by Assyria in 722 B.C., and the Jews there were killed or assimilated into Assyrian culture. They are sometimes referred to as the 10 lost tribes of Israel, because they were never heard from again.

The southern kingdom, Judah, saw what happened to the northern kingdom, and repented when God was threatening to destroy them as well. This worked for a while but they were eventually overcome by the same sins and corruption as the northern kingdom. God sent them prophet after prophet to try and call them to repent and return to God's ways, but they also refused.

Finally, with no other options open for him, God was forced to call the nation of Babylon against the southern kingdom of Judah to destroy it; and they did in 587/586 B.C. The Babylonians took the Jews back to Babylon to live in exile. After about 70 years, the Persians defeated the Babylonians and allowed the Jews to return to Jerusalem and their homeland.

When the Jews returned home, they were back in their land.

But gone were the days when they used to rule themselves.

They longed for the days of the united kingdom of Israel, when they had their own power, politics, king, and country. Now they were surviving in their homeland, but as powerless subjects of the superpower of their day. When they returned home, the Persian Empire continued to rule and reign over them, then the Greeks, then the most powerful of all: the Romans.

This was the setting when Jesus came on the scene.

The longing of the Jewish people was to somehow return to the good ol' days of the past, when they had their own king and country, all based in Jerusalem. In fact, God had even promised through some of their prophets that he would eventually restore the kingdom of Israel and give it a new king to lead it.

They longed for the day when they thought God was going to re-establish his reign on the earth, and God had promised he was going to do it through the new king he was going to send.

Do you know what they called that hoped-for king?

Messiah.

Which is *Christos* in Greek, and *Christ* in English.

It was revolutionary language that meant God was about to fulfill all these promises.

But the Jewish people incorrectly thought the messiah would do this by leading and winning a violent war against Rome, and then they would live forever with the messiah on the earth. At that time, they believed all the faithful Jews would be raised bodily from the dead and live with them forever on the earth under the eternal reign of the messiah.

This was what Jews referred to when they talked about the kingdom of God.

It was language of violent and explosive wars of revolution.

This was the scene when Jesus showed up proclaiming the kingdom of God was near.

But his Jewish listeners would have understood that as a highly anticipated call to arms. For them, it was a call to war and violent rebellion against Rome, their hated enemy. It was a call to kill and destroy in the name of their God. They thought the messiah was going to defeat their enemies by defeating the Romans, and that he was going to do this through all out bloody warfare.

But that was the exact opposite kind of revolution Jesus was leading.

So, Jesus needed to be very careful that his fellow Jews didn't misunderstand him by thinking he was calling them to make war against the Romans. This is why Jesus spends so much time talking about the kingdom of God. In fact, he talks about it more than any other topic. [3] He tells story after story about it so his followers will understand how radically different his definition of the kingdom of God is from that of his fellow Jews.

Jesus says the enemies he came to destroy are not the Romans, but Satan, sin, and death itself.

He says that even the chosen Jewish people need to be rescued from these things.

Because they are just as lost and blind as the pagan non-Jewish gentiles.

He says the revolution he is leading and inviting us into is the exact opposite of all the violent revolutions of hatred and revenge that human history is full of.

The revolution he is leading is based on the same self-sacrificial, non-violent enemy-love that he demonstrated and taught during his entire ministry. And then, after he was crucified and raised from the dead, he sends out his followers to continue his work of proclaiming and demonstrating that God has launched a kingdom that's as far from the violent revolutions of war and death as anything can be.

In light of this, I would argue that followers of Jesus fall into the same violent trap that most of Jesus's Jewish contemporaries did. This happens every time we support violence or wars, and every time we think we can defeat our enemies by defeating human beings—who are not our enemies. [4] To the extent that we do this, we must all repent and return to the kingdom vision of the man we claim to follow.

The Spirit of the Lord Is Upon Me

Towards the beginning of Luke's Gospel, we read this about Jesus:

> *When he came to Nazareth, where he had been brought up, he went*
> *to the synagogue on the sabbath day, as was his custom. He stood up*
> *to read, and the scroll of the prophet Isaiah was given to him. He*
> *unrolled the scroll and found the place where it was written:*
>
> *"The Spirit of the Lord is upon me, because he has anointed me to*
> *bring good news to the poor. He has sent me to proclaim release to the*
> *captives and recovery of sight to the blind, to let the oppressed go free,*
> *to proclaim the year of the Lord's favor."*
>
> *And he rolled up the scroll, gave it back to the attendant, and sat*
> *down. The eyes of all in the synagogue were fixed on him. Then he*
> *began to say to them, "Today this scripture has been fulfilled in your*
> *hearing."* [5]

The fact that Jesus proclaimed these words from the prophet Isaiah, which was written hundreds of years before Jesus, shows how much the good news (the Gospel) of Jesus fulfills, reflects, and culminates the good news of Isaiah. Jesus is showing that his ministry fits like a glove among the ancient Jewish prophetic tradition.

He is saying that his good news is the same as what the prophet Isaiah announced centuries earlier: the good news of the kingdom of God.

And, according to both Isaiah and Jesus, when the good news of the kingdom of God is proclaimed, it means good news for the poor, release for the captives in bondage, recovery of (spiritual) sight for the (spiritually) blind, and freedom for the oppressed.

In fact, this is what Jesus's entire ministry is about.

That's why Jesus says these words of Isaiah were fulfilled when he read them.

What does Jesus mean by that?

He means that Jesus has taken them to where they were pointing the whole time.

Jesus announced these things, and then did them during the next three years of ministry. He actually did all those things so his fellow Jews could see that the story God had been writing for more than 1,000 years with Israel was finally coming to its culmination.

In Jesus, all the Jewish scriptures were being fulfilled, as he took the Jewish story where it had been moving and pointing the entire time. When Jesus told the people in the synagogue that verse by Isaiah had been fulfilled, he wasn't lying.

God's story is written in human history and scripture, and all of us can read it and get swept up into it. In fact, God didn't need to do this, but he graciously invited us to play a small role in his drama—the great drama of human history.

This would be like having a masterful director like Steven Spielberg ask you or me if we want to be in his next movie, even though we have no qualifications as actors, and he certainly doesn't need us to finish it. I would jump at the chance, and that's what Jesus hopes the Jewish audience in that synagogue will do when he says these words.

That's also what Jesus hopes everyone who reads them will do.

Not Everyone Who Says Lord Lord Will Enter

We've established that Jesus was the savior—the messiah. But just because we proclaim his name doesn't necessarily mean we're saved. Jesus, himself, said this, and I confess that these words of Jesus are, for me, some of the most terrifying words in all of scripture.

Here, at the end of the Sermon on the Mount, which is all about the kinds of actions Jesus expects his followers to take, he says that not everyone who calls on him will enter into his kingdom. Here is the passage, along with the paragraph before and after, so we can see why he said this:

> Beware of false prophets, who come to you in sheep's clothing but inwardly are ravenous wolves. You will know them by their fruits. Are grapes gathered from thorns, or figs from thistles? In the same way, every good tree bears good fruit, but the bad tree bears bad fruit. A good tree cannot bear bad fruit, nor can a bad tree bear good fruit. Every tree that does not bear good fruit is cut down and thrown into the fire. Thus you will know them by their fruits.
>
> Not everyone who says to me, "Lord, Lord," will enter the kingdom of heaven, but only the one who does the will of my Father in heaven. On that day many will say to me, "Lord, Lord, did we not prophesy in your name, and cast out demons in your name, and do many deeds of power in your name?" Then I will declare to them, "I never knew you; go away from me, you evildoers."

Everyone then who hears these words of mine and acts on them will be like a wise man who built his house on rock. The rain fell, the floods came, and the winds blew and beat on that house, but it did not fall, because it had been founded on rock. And everyone who hears these words of mine and does not act on them will be like a foolish man who built his house on sand. The rain fell, and the floods came, and the winds blew and beat against that house, and it fell—and great was its fall! [6]

These verses sum up the longest single teaching Jesus gives in the New Testament, and they're all about what his followers are supposed to do. They are about how we are supposed to act and live. The first paragraph talks about knowing false prophets by their fruits, just like you know trees from their fruit. By fruit, Jesus is referring to the external and visible actions of the people he's talking about.

This is made clear once again in paragraph three, where Jesus says the only difference between the wise man and the fool is that the wise man hears Jesus's words and does them, while the fool hears his words and doesn't do them. Both men hear and know what Jesus commands them to do, but only one man does it.

These two related themes of putting the words and teaching of Jesus into action should help us understand what Jesus says in the middle.

Jesus says there will be people who call him Lord, but who won't enter into his kingdom.

There will even be people who prophesy.

And cast out demons in his name.

But they will not enter.

Jesus hints as to why they will not enter but he doesn't directly say it: the people don't know him. I would argue that knowing Jesus in this context means to know his teaching and will for human beings, and to put it into practice in our own lives. This is what Jesus talks about for the three preceding chapters that lead up to these words.

It's also what separates the wise man from the fool: both men have and know the commands of Jesus, but only one of them does them. That means we're not saved by merely knowing intellectually about the words of Jesus, or by memorizing them.

We're saved by doing them.

That's what knowing Jesus means in this context.

That's also what this whole section is about.

When Jesus talks about people who call him Lord but who won't enter into his kingdom, he is talking about people who call him Lord but who don't actually put his teachings into practice. They call him Lord but don't do what he said. Instead, their lives and actions are like the rotten fruit of the false prophets, or like the fool in the analogy of the houses, both of which lead to destruction.

If this is true, then the best way for us to avoid being the people who call Jesus Lord with our lips only is to put the ethical teachings and commands of Jesus into practice. After all, Matthew devoted the preceding three chapters to recording all the ethical commands Jesus just unloaded for anyone who wants to follow him.

And we need to do them.

It's really that simple.

We need to make peace.

We need to love and pray for our enemies.

We need to forgive without end.

We need to seek reconciliation.

We need to turn the other cheek.

We need to humble ourselves.

We need to serve others before we serve ourselves.

We need to serve the least and last in our society.

We need to refuse to respond to evil with evil.

We need to love with the same self-sacrificial, non-violent enemy-love of Jesus.

We need to back up our words with our actions.

How can you do these things to the people in your world?

2

THE I AM STATEMENTS

The *I Am* statements of Jesus are radical and revolutionary because they link together God's name and identity in the Old Testament with the person of Jesus in the New Testament. Shockingly, Jesus uses this structure to identify himself with the God revealed in the Old Testament. No founder or leader of any major religion has ever claimed to be divine (they usually act as messengers), but with these statements, Jesus does exactly that. This is totally unique in the history of religions, and it also got Jesus into lots of trouble with the Jewish religious leaders of his day. Nothing could be more revolutionary than that, so let's take a look for ourselves.

I Am the Bread of Life

The *I am* statements of Jesus are fascinating and revolutionary, but I need to give some background so we can fully understand how Jesus uses them.

Jesus doesn't just use them randomly without thinking. All of the claims he makes using that structure are pre-meditated and completely thought-out and planned.

Nothing about these statements is left to chance.

In Exodus 3:13-15, God reveals his name to human beings for the first time in human history. God tells Moses that his name is *I am who I am,* which can also be translated as *I will be who I will be.* Then God says his name is *YHWH*, which is a name based on the Hebrew verb *to be.*

But since Jews refuse to say the name of God (which is *YHWH*) out of respect for him, when they come across the divine name *YHWH*, they say "*The Lord*" because that's what he is. *YHWH*, the God of Israel, is *the lord* of all of creation, so when Jews read *YHWH* in their scriptures (what Christians call the Old Testament), they say *The LORD.*

And to clarify that they are talking about *YHWH* instead of some lesser lord, the Jewish people write the word *lord* in all capitals, as *LORD.* That means every time we read *The LORD* in the Old Testament, the Hebrew text actually says *YHWH,* which is the covenant name of God. So, when God says *I am* in the Old Testament, he is identifying himself as his identity and name: *he is the one who is.*

He is the eternal one.

He is the one without beginning or end.

And Jesus implies this background when he makes his *I am* statements in the New Testament. The first one in the Gospel of John is this:

I am the bread of life. Whoever comes to me will never be hungry, and whoever believes in me will never be thirsty. But I said to you that you have seen me and yet do not believe. Everything that the Father gives me will come to me, and anyone who comes to me I will never drive away; for I have come down from heaven, not to do my own will, but the will of him who sent me. [7]

When Jesus says he's the *bread of life,* he is referring to the manna that miraculously appeared in order to sustain and save the Jewish people as they were wandering in the desert. [8] Just as manna appeared as a divine act to save the Jewish people, so, too, has Jesus appeared by divine act to save the Jewish people, and in fact the whole world.

But there's a difference between Jesus and the manna: the ancient Jews who ate manna were hungry again soon after eating. After all, it was food that God provided miraculously, but at the end of the day that's all it was: food to help them survive. Jesus, on the other hand, says in these verses that whoever comes to him to eat and drink will never be hungry or thirsty again.

How can this be? Because Jesus is referring to spiritual hunger and thirst. He's saying that if we are spiritually hungry and thirsty, and if we come to him to be filled, then he will give us what we long for: permanent spiritual satisfaction and fulfillment.

As someone who went through that process with Jesus, I can vouch for these words. I was never in danger of going hungry or thirsty physically, but all the years of partying and searching for meaning, purpose, and joy led me to nothing and left me with tons of spiritual hunger and thirst.

I thought I could find joy in the life of partying, but I was wrong.

I thought I could find happiness in the life of partying, but I was wrong.

I thought I could find purpose and meaning in the life of partying, but I was wrong.

My soul and spirit longed for something to give my life meaning, but nothing in that world could deliver what I hoped for. So, after years of living that way, I turned to the only place I hadn't tried:

I turned to God.

I turned to Jesus.

And that was when my real life began.

My soul and spirit were so hungry and thirsty that once I found Jesus, I ate and drank every part of him I could get.

I needed him.

I wanted him.

And since finding the true source of spiritual nourishment, I've never been spiritually hungry or thirsty again.

I'm hungry and thirsty for more of him, but that's all.

So how will you respond to these radical words of Jesus?

I Am the Light of the World

The next *I am* statement of Jesus comes in chapter eight, when he says he's the light of the world. Here are his words: *"I am the light of the world. Whoever follows me will never walk in darkness but will have the light of life." [9]*

These words are intriguing because, in the Gospel of Matthew, Jesus says to his disciples: *you are the light of the world.* [10] Which is it? Is Jesus the light of the world or are his followers the light of the world? The answer is: both, but in very different ways.

I'm going to make this point by asking you (my reader) a question:

Is the moon bright?

Think about it for a few seconds.

The answer to that question is: *no, the moon isn't bright.* In fact, the moon is dark. It produces no light. But if that's true, then why does it look so bright when we go outside at night and see more light coming from it than from anything else shining in the sky? In fact, I've surfed many times at night during full moons because there's more than enough light to surf.

If the moon is dark, then why does it appear so bright?

The moon doesn't produce or make its own light.

Instead, it reflects the light that emits from the sun.

The moon appears bright because it's like a huge mirror hanging up in the sky.

This is a perfect analogy of how both Jesus and his followers are the light of the world.

The followers of Jesus are the light of the world in the same way the moon lights up the night sky. We don't produce light in and of ourselves. By ourselves, we are just as dark, lost, and corrupt as everyone else. But when we shine the light of Jesus through our lives and out to the dark world, people see our lives contrast the darkness and are drawn to the source of the light, Jesus.

Every time we forgive someone instead of trying to get even, the dark world can see the light of Jesus in us.

Every time we love and pray for our enemies, deny ourselves, or put others before ourselves, our lives reflect the light of Jesus into the darkness.

Every time we take up the cause of the hungry, the weak, and the broken people of our world, we shine the light of Jesus through our lives into the darkness.

Every time we seek healing and restoration instead of revenge and retaliation, we shine the light of Jesus into the darkness.

Jesus is the source of the light we shine, and without him, we would be just as dark and lost as everyone else. Let's keep that in mind so we don't think too highly of ourselves in this process. Our goal is to shine like the moon so the dark world can see us reflect the light of love, healing, redemption, salvation, and restoration that only Jesus can offer.

And that's just about the most exciting thing I can think of spending my life doing!

How can you shine the light of Jesus into the darkness of your world?

I Am the Gate and the Good Shepherd

The *I am* statements about the gate and the good shepherd go hand in hand, so I'll address them together:

> So again Jesus said to them, "Very truly, I tell you, I am the gate for the sheep. All who came before me are thieves and bandits; but the sheep did not listen to them. I am the gate. Whoever enters by me will be saved, and will come in and go out and find pasture. The thief comes only to steal and kill and destroy. I came that they may have life, and have it abundantly.
>
> I am the good shepherd. The good shepherd lays down his life for the sheep. The hired hand, who is not the shepherd and does not own the sheep, sees the wolf coming and leaves the sheep and runs away—and the wolf snatches them and scatters them. The hired hand runs away because a hired hand does not care for the sheep. I am the good shepherd. I know my own and my own know me, just as the Father knows me and I know the Father. And I lay down my life for the sheep. I have other sheep that do not belong to this fold. I must bring them also, and they will listen to my voice. So there will be one flock, one shepherd. For this reason the Father loves me, because I lay down my life in order to take it up again. No one takes it from me, but I lay it down of my own accord. I have power to lay it down, and I have power to take it up again. I have received this command from my Father. [11]

When Jesus says he is the gate, he is referring to the gate that serves to enclose sheep within a protective barrier. Normally this would be some kind of fence with a door in it, so the sheep can go out through the door to find pastures and eat, but then enter back through it to stay within the protective walls of the enclosure.

When Jesus says he is the gate, he is saying that he's the one we need to pass through to live.

After all, we need to pass through him as we go out to find spiritual nourishment, but we pass through again on our way back in, and use him to protect our lives into eternity. And just like there is only one door, only Jesus can protect and sustain us in the ways we need it. If we go to anyone or anything else, we will learn that only Jesus can give us those things.

When Jesus says he is the good shepherd, he is saying that he lays his life down for his sheep.

This pre-shadows the death Jesus ultimately suffered, but he really did lay down his life for his sheep—you, me, and every human being who has ever lived. I love how Jesus says he knows his sheep and his sheep know him, and that we will listen to his voice. After all, that's exactly what we're doing right now as we make our way through this book together.

I and the Father Are One

These statements, and others like them, are among the most scandalous words Jesus ever said. With these words, Jesus claims to be divine:

> *The Father and I are one . . . the Father is in me and I am in the Father.* [12]

When Jesus makes claims that are this radical, there are only three possibilities of how we can respond, which were originally conceived brilliantly by the great C. S. Lewis:

1. He is knowingly lying through his teeth.
2. He is a lunatic, and as crazy as anyone can be, to think he's actually God when he really isn't.
3. He is telling the truth.

That's it.

Those are the only three options available to us.

If Jesus is lying, then he's a pathological liar who is making insanely crazy claims about his identity that he knows to be false. But I ask you this: do all the incredibly wise and loving words and actions of Jesus seem like the kind of things a pathological liar would say and do? I would say no, so I can't believe the first option.

Likewise, if Jesus was insane, to the point where he thought he was God but wasn't, then would we expect to read about all his incredibly wise and profound words and actions in the Gospels? I don't think so.

Likewise, how on earth would Jesus be able to do the mind-boggling supernatural signs and miracles that were witnessed by thousands of people if he were only a deranged crazy person? When the people gave clear testimony about Jesus healing them, were they all crazy as well? That also seems impossible, and therefore we should reject that option, too.

If the first two options don't apply to Jesus, then we must apply the third one:

Jesus was telling the truth.

And if that's true, then the only proper thing to do is fall down at his feet and call him lord. As someone who has done that very thing, I can tell you firsthand that it will be the best decision you ever make.

Life won't suddenly be easy, but you will discover a sense of joy, purpose, and meaning you could never attain separate from Jesus. Knowing we have the ultimate victory in him also helps us when we're going through tough times and feel like we can barely make it.

There is another point I want to make about these astonishing words: these are what set Jesus apart from every other leader and founder of all the major religions of the world.

Those people claimed to be human messengers and prophets sent by God, but only Jesus claimed to be God.

None of those people claimed to be divine.

Only Jesus did.

That makes Christianity completely unique among the world's religions.

Ancient Judaism was started and mediated by Moses, who was a normal human and made no claims of divinity. Buddhism was started by Buddha, who was a normal person and made no divine claims. Confucius was a normal person who never made claims of divinity, and the same can be said for the Prophet Mohammed, who started Islam. Even modern religions, like Mormonism, fall into this category, since it was started by Joseph Smith, who made no divine claims.

I make this point so you can see that only Jesus Christ made the very bold claim to be divine.

And I ask you: if he wasn't divine, then how did he get such amazing wisdom, brilliance, insight, and power? Since thousands of people personally witnessed his healings, miracles, and supernatural acts of power, he didn't do those things while hiding in some random cave with no one else to corroborate what he did.

He did them out in the open where literally everyone else could see what he did.

No one could deny his power because they saw it.

No one could deny his authority because they witnessed it.

In fact, this is one of the reasons Christianity exploded so quickly.

Jesus didn't tell people he had some vision in a dream that no one can check or verify, like the leaders of all the other major religions. Instead, he spoke with brilliance and insight that could only be from divine sources, and he healed so many people out in public that no one could deny his supernatural power to heal.

In fact, even the Jewish religious leaders who were against Jesus were forced to recognize his power to heal supernaturally. They never tried to argue that Jesus didn't heal people supernaturally. They knew everyone had seen him do it, and many of them witnessed him do it. So instead of trying to deny the power everyone knew Jesus had, they attacked him by insisting that his power came from Satan, and not from God. [13]

As proof that he is in fact from God, Jesus confronts their error by saying a house divided against itself will never stand. When even the enemies of Jesus are forced to recognize his supernatural power and authority to heal, it's a pretty convincing argument that Jesus was, in fact, divine. [14]

That may sound crazy.

But it's the most logical, reasonable explanation of the historical facts.

How will you respond?

If you take this step and recognize this, then the only proper response is to call Jesus lord of your life.

What else could he do to prove his identity to you?

Be raised from the dead? Well, he did that too!

I Am the Resurrection and the Life

At one point, Jesus says these stunning words: *"I am the resurrection and the life. Those who believe in me, even though they die, will live, and everyone who lives and believes in me will never die."* [15]

We need to unpack this to understand what Jesus is talking about when he says he is the resurrection. From these verses and others like them, we see that, at a minimum, resurrection includes eternal life; we will live forever with Jesus. [16] At minimum, it gives us the hope and assurance that we will be reunited with brothers and sisters in the faith for eternity.

My friend once posted a picture on Facebook of the moment his son returned home from traveling through Europe alone for months. He took a picture of the exact moment his son hugged his mom for the first time in months, and then posted it with the title of hoping that heaven will be an extended version of that moment of reuniting with loved ones.

I thought it was an absolutely perfect and brilliant way to capture the deep sense of love and community that awaits everyone who has the chance to be part of it.

In fact, I think about that aspect of eternal life often. My severely disabled younger brother passed away one night in his sleep about 13 years ago, and I constantly long to be reunited with him. Likewise, my dad just passed away a few months ago, and I have been reminded of how much I can't wait to see him. I can honestly say that I long for those days, and sometimes that hope keeps me going when things get hard.

But now I want to go into the deep-end of resurrection, so we can really understand what Jesus is saying.

Resurrection is much more than just eternal life. Resurrection means we are raised bodily in the future with a glorified and perfected version of the bodies we have now. [17] Our bodies will be raised just like the body of Jesus, whose resurrection body still had the wounds from his crucifixion.

Resurrection means we will live forever, but not as most Christians tend to think of heaven: disembodied souls floating around in some strange foreign place apart from the earth.

That mistaken idea is nothing but Greek Platonic philosophy.

Not biblical theology.

That is a Greek view that has no support anywhere in scripture, which has always insisted that bodily resurrection will happen on the renewed earth.

The world's premier New Testament scholar, N.T. Wright, says that when we die now, we go immediately to be with God. Most Christians mistakenly think of it like a one-way ticket away from the earth, but scripture is clear that when we die we go to the presence of God (wherever that is); but that trip is a round-trip ticket because we will be raised bodily to live forever on the earth with God when he establishes his kingdom in fullness on the earth. [18]

I want to make one more point about living the eternal life of the resurrection:

Resurrection life doesn't begin after we die and go to be with God.

For followers of Jesus, it begins now.

We are called to be a community of people who don't live by the ways of the decaying world we live in. Instead, we're called to live the resurrection life of the kingdom of God now, in the midst of this life. We're called to show this corrupt world a portrait of the perfectly just and whole kingdom of God that we're going to dwell in forever.

There's not going to be death, murder, killing, violence, hatred, insults, racism, criticism, bigotry, and oppression in the eternal kingdom of God. Therefore, followers of Jesus are called to put those old ways behind us right now, living out the values and qualities of God's kingdom.

This is, once again, why it's completely inappropriate for

followers of Jesus to kill or attack people.

Or to get revenge.

When we do things like that, we are living as the people we used to be.

We are living according to the old ways of a decaying world.

We forget that, in Jesus, we are new creations.

And Jesus calls us to put away those harmful destructive ways forever.

Similarly, instead of living out those negative things, we are now called to embrace and live out the things that will last forever in the kingdom of God: self-sacrificial love, forgiveness, peace, non-violence, restoration, healing, reconciliation, and redemption.

Followers of Jesus who fall back into the old destructive ways have forgotten who their lord is.

They have forgotten who they are.

I Am the Way, the Truth, and the Life

During his last night with his disciples, Jesus started to tell them how he would soon be going away to prepare a place for them. Then Thomas said they didn't know where he was going, so they wouldn't be able to find him. Jesus responded with these words:

> *I am the way, and the truth, and the life. No one comes to the Father except through me. If you know me, you will know my Father also. From now on you do know him and have seen him.* [19]

These are extremely profound and loaded words. Jesus is saying he is the truth about the Father. He is saying that he is the true way to the Father—and to everlasting life in the kingdom of God. Jesus is saying that his followers don't need to do some weird or unexpected thing to come to God. Instead, all they need to do is come to Jesus.

He is saying that all his followers need to do to find the true way to God is keep following him. We're good as long as we're following the way of Jesus. We don't need to go do some weird religious task in order to have access to God. All we need is Jesus, and if we have him, then we have everything we need.

Likewise, people who aren't following Jesus, or the true way of Jesus, are in danger of not getting access to eternal life with God. Jesus is the only way, which means there are no other ways to God or to eternal life with him in his kingdom. This is why Jesus says no one comes to the Father except through him. [20] He is the only true way to eternal life with God in the kingdom of God.

This seems scandalous.

But it's true.

Because only Jesus defeated death for us by dying and being raised three days later to prove to everyone that what he was saying was true; and only Jesus launched the beginning of the culmination of the story God has written across history.

Therefore, only Jesus is deserving of our lives.

Only Jesus is deserving of our praise.

Only Jesus is deserving of our gratitude.

Only Jesus is deserving of our appreciation.

Only Jesus is deserving of our devotion.

Only Jesus is deserving of our faith.

Only Jesus is deserving of our admiration.

Only Jesus is deserving of our loyalty.

Only Jesus is deserving.

I Am the True Vine

A little later on the last night Jesus spent with his disciples, he told them these profound words:

> *I am the true vine, and my Father is the vinegrower. He removes every branch in me that bears no fruit. Every branch that bears fruit he prunes to make it bear more fruit. You have already been cleansed by the word that I have spoken to you. Abide in me as I abide in you. Just as the branch cannot bear fruit by itself unless it abides in the vine, neither can you unless you abide in me. I am the vine, you are the branches. Those who abide in me and I in them bear much fruit, because apart from me you can do nothing. Whoever does not abide in me is thrown away like a branch and withers; such branches are gathered, thrown into the fire, and burned. If you abide in me, and my words abide in you, ask for whatever you wish, and it will be done for you. My Father is glorified by this, that you bear much fruit and become my disciples. [21]*

Jesus starts out by saying he is the true vine, and that God the Father is the one who grows the vines. The Father removes all the branches in him that don't bear fruit, like a master gardener prunes trees by cutting off dead and unhealthy branches, so the whole tree bears more fruit. My in-laws are master gardeners who are constantly out in the garden, pruning and trimming the bushes, flowers, and trees for exactly this purpose: to produce more fruit and flowers.

Later, Jesus says we (meaning his followers) are the fruit and he is the branch, and he states the obvious truth that branches can't produce fruit on their own. They need to be connected to the vine, or the trunk of a tree, in order to survive and produce fruit. If a branch is cut off from the vine, then it will die and be thrown out. That means we, the followers of Jesus, can only survive and thrive if we keep ourselves connected to him, the vine.

How do we do that?

We abide with him.

We spend time with him.

We seek him and his will.

We read about him.

We listen to him.

And then we do what he tells us.

That brings us to another point: what does it look like to bear fruit? What part of our lives is Jesus talking about when he tells us to bear fruit? How do we do it? Fruit is always something exposed visibly for everyone to see, just like the fruit of a tree is exposed for everyone to see. But just as the fruit of a tree can be good or bad, so, too, can our fruit be good or bad. What is our fruit?

Our fruit is our actions.

It's what we do.

And they're exposed for everyone to see.

So when Jesus says he wants us to bear good fruit, he's saying he wants us to produce good works and actions that everyone can see. No matter where people look at our lives, or what setting they see us in, they should see us demonstrating the good fruit of things like self-sacrificial love, compassion, empathy, justice, fairness, truth, faithfulness, peace, non-violence, forgiveness, reconciliation, and joy.

This is what it means to bear fruit.

This is what it means to abide in Jesus.

This is what it means to stay connected to the vine.

Because the minute we try to do these things apart from Jesus is the moment we start to wither up and die.

So what kinds of fruit are you producing?

If you are producing the bad fruit of things like hatred, anger, violence, destruction, racism, sexism, oppression, hostility, arrogance, ignorance, pride, envy, and jealousy, then it's time to repent and return to the vine.

Those things do not describe Jesus, and they shouldn't describe followers of Jesus.

So if they describe you, then it's time to return to Jesus.

It's time to abide in the vine.

It's time to produce good fruit.

Ask Jesus to show you how.

Then listen.

And, finally, do it.

3

NOT ALL-KNOWING OR ALL-POWERFUL

Anyone who reads scripture carefully will realize that Jesus didn't know everything, but this contradicts what most Christians believe about him—that he was omnipotent and omniscient, just like God. While God may be omniscient and omnipotent, however you define those terms, it is obvious that Jesus was not, and that totally changes the way I view him. In fact, it leads me to appreciate him even more than I would if he were omniscient or omnipotent. [22] Instead of coming to earth as an all-powerful, all-knowing, fully divine god, Jesus took the form of a normal human who, like the rest of us, was limited. How radical is that?

No One Knows When Jesus Will Return

At one point in the Gospel of Matthew, Jesus says this about the time of his return: *"But about that day and hour no one knows, neither the angels of heaven, nor the Son, but only the Father."* [23]

This is simply amazing.

Jesus says no one will know the time of his return.

Which includes the angels.

And even the son.

Which is him.

So even Jesus didn't know the time of his own return!

According to him, only the Father knows.

This blows my mind.

I can't fathom how Jesus wouldn't know the time of his own return, but I need to believe it since he's the one who said it. What does that mean for those of us who are followers of Jesus?

First: millions of Christians make claims all the time about knowing when Jesus will return. In fact, the whole theology of dispensationalism, which was invented in the 1800's and is based on predicting a supposed rapture when Jesus returns, is completely flawed because it's based on trying to predict the very thing Jesus says no one can predict. Dispensationalism is hugely popular, with all its crazy end-time rapture theories. But, according to these words of Jesus, no one can know the time of his return, so it's a waste to try and predict it.

How then should we respond?

That brings me to my second point: Jesus immediately follows up these words with a story about being ready when he returns, and that's what he wants us to focus on. [24] Instead of wasting so much time and energy trying to predict when Jesus will return, which as we can see is impossible, followers of Jesus should focus our energy on doing what Jesus calls us to do. We should do what

Jesus said so we won't get caught doing something inappropriate when he returns.

That is as far as we should go into speculations about when Jesus is going to return, which means all the rapture and end-time enthusiasts should stop wasting their time trying to predict something they can't predict. I can't tell you how many ministries are set up to try and predict when Jesus will return, but, according to Jesus, they're wasting their time.

These kinds of Christians should stop wasting money and resources on these pointless efforts, and redirect them to what we should really be doing: caring for the sick and vulnerable, helping to feed and clothe the hungry and homeless, visiting the prisoners in jail, and supporting ministries that help people heal from addictions and all kinds of harmful conditions. [25]

Jesus Asks If It's Possible to Take His Cup of Suffering

At one point, when Jesus knows he is about to be arrested and crucified, he is overwhelmed with fear and goes away to pray with his three closest friends:

> He took with him Peter and the two sons of Zebedee, and began to be grieved and agitated. Then he said to them, "I am deeply grieved, even to death; remain here, and stay awake with me." And going a little farther, he threw himself on the ground and prayed, "My Father, if it is possible, let this cup pass from me; yet not what I want but what you want." Then he came to the disciples and found them sleeping; and he said to Peter, "So, could you not stay awake with me one hour? Stay awake and pray that you may not come into the time of trial; the spirit indeed is willing, but the flesh is weak." Again he

went away for the second time and prayed, "My Father, if this cannot pass unless I drink it, your will be done." Again he came and found them sleeping, for their eyes were heavy. So leaving them again, he went away and prayed for the third time, saying the same words. [26]

A few things stand out to me about this.

First: Jesus is terrified and grieved to the point of death. He's not faking. He knows about the suffering he's going to endure and it terrifies him. This was not something he wanted to go through, and he made that very clear to his Father in this prayer, but he did it anyway because he realized there was no other way. Jesus is on the verge of breaking down because of his fear and anguish.

Second: Jesus prays that his cup of suffering be taken from him *if it is possible,* which means Jesus doesn't know everything and certainly doesn't know if it's possible for him to save the world without being crucified. [27] Although he's ready to go through with it if there's no other way, he hopes it's possible to avoid the suffering. But he's not sure if it is, so he asks his Father.

Third: In this interaction we see Jesus ask for something from his Father, but his Father says *no.* That means we see Jesus live out exactly what we experience when we ask God for something but his answer is not what we want. Jesus has to trust in the goodness of his Father, even when he doesn't get the answer he wants, just like we do. This makes me appreciate what Jesus did for us in a whole new way.

For example, growing up, we prayed for my younger disabled brother to be healed but he never was. In the past couple years, I also found out I have an incurable disease called Huntington's

Disease. We also prayed for me to be healed and were disappointed that God didn't do it.

This kind of negative answer from God is always hard to deal with, and, to be honest, I don't fully understand why God doesn't heal more. [28] I have friends who have been cured of HIV and Fiber Myalgia, which are both incurable, so I know it does happen.

But I also know that's the exception.

Not the norm.

Yet, just because something is the norm doesn't mean it's easy to deal with. It's not. What I love about these verses is they show Jesus pleading with his Father about allowing him to avoid all the pain and suffering if there is another way to save the world; and in this situation God gives even Jesus the answer Jesus didn't want.

Jesus wanted to avoid the pain and suffering if there was another way to save the world.

But there wasn't.

So he composed himself and took it like the man he was.

He learned there was no other way.

Not this time.

When God doesn't answer my prayers like I want him to, it helps me to know that even Jesus experienced that. But, like Jesus, we can still be faithful to our calling and trust in God's goodness, even when sometimes we don't completely understand it.

What are the ways God has not answered your prayers?

What are the ways he has let you down?

Just know that even Jesus experienced that.

I believe that God often does this to teach us something greater and deeper.

What is he trying to teach you? What has he been trying to teach you as you look back over the disappointment in your life? I realized that God taught me many things by not healing my younger brother, and by not healing me of Huntington's. It hasn't been easy, and at times I have been angry at him, but over time I began to see that his will for me was bigger and greater than those two prayers.

Just like God's will for Jesus was greater and bigger than what Jesus asked for in his prayer.

Jesus wanted to avoid suffering, if it were possible, to save the world.

But God was planning on saving the world through Jesus's suffering.

When Jesus realized there was no other way, he finally gave in to his Father's will, but that took him some time. I admire him because from then on, he doesn't waiver at all. Jesus shows us all how to live through answers from God that we don't want. He finally accepts it and then commits himself to following his Father's plan and will.

I think this is a perfect example for us to follow.

When we inevitably ask God for something and don't receive it, we don't need to abandon God or think he must not exist. Instead, like Jesus, we should come to terms with God's will for our life, and have the courage and strength to fully embrace our situation and reality. When we ask for something and don't get it, we need to look to Jesus to learn how to adapt to God's will and step completely into it.

My God My God, Why Have You Forsaken Me?

When Jesus was crucified, he yelled one of the most shocking and unexpected things we could ever imagine:

> When it was noon, darkness came over the whole land until three in the afternoon. At three o'clock Jesus cried out with a loud voice, "Eloi, Eloi, lema sabachthani?" which means, "My God, my God, why have you forsaken me?" [29]

Jesus's haunting cry and question make me realize a couple things. First: he really was feeling all the pain and anguish of the crucifixion. This truly was God on the cross, and he wasn't shielded from the pain and anguish of it in any way. That means that when we find ourselves suffering, we know Jesus has walked in our steps; he knows what it's like to be beaten to a pulp.

That also means he can help us get through whatever we go through—if we ask him. [30]

Jesus was not shielded from the kind of pain and suffering we all experience every day. God didn't want to remove Jesus from his suffering because he had a greater and bigger purpose for him in going through it.

That encourages me because I often feel like Jesus and wonder where is God's will? Here, Jesus shows us that sometimes God's will is for us to go through the pain and suffering. It's not fun, but when we do, we learn things we could never have learned any other way. [31]

Second: Jesus experiences, for the first time, the sin of the world. He feels forsaken by God because, amazingly, in that moment, for the first time ever, he is. God turned his back on him, as Jesus acted as the personal concentration of all the sin and evil human beings have ever done.

I think all the murder, killing, rape, and horrible sins that human beings have ever done were somehow personalized in Jesus at this moment.

Can you imagine how horrible and terrifying that must have felt?

So God turned his back on his son.

For the first time ever.

God withdrew his presence from him.

For the first time ever.

God forsook him.

For the first time ever.

But why would Jesus submit himself to that? [32]

To reach and save you and I.

Can I get an amen?

II

THE RELIGIOUS CONTRARIAN

4

DEATH OF RELIGION

Jesus was so radical that he virtually killed religion. He overthrew all the religious systems that were designed to keep normal people separate from God. Temples and priests were designed to keep ordinary people from God, not bring them closer; but Jesus destroyed that whole system of worship and adoration. Instead, he gave us direct access to God's presence and spirit. But as we will see, human beings couldn't handle this direct access, so we created our own Christianized version of the religions that Jesus had already killed.

One time, when the Jewish religious leaders at the temple confronted Jesus about what he was doing, he responded to them with a story about two sons that ended with these words:

Truly I tell you, the tax collectors and the prostitutes are going into the kingdom of God ahead of you. For John came to you in the way of righteousness and you did not believe him, but the tax collectors and

the prostitutes believed him; and even after you saw it, you did not
change your minds and believe him. [33]

These are stunning words, especially when we think about the
fact that Jesus is speaking to the Jewish religious leaders of his
day. Faithful Jews looked at tax collectors and prostitutes as the
scum of the earth, so these were very inflammatory words for
Jesus to say to anyone, but especially to these Jewish religious
leaders.

Tax collectors were the one group of people the Jews probably
hated more than the Romans. They were Jewish people who had
betrayed their own Jewish flesh and blood to go work for the
Romans. They collected taxes from the Jews to give to the
Romans, so Jews despised them and pretty much thought they
were less than human.

In fact, tax collectors could keep all the money they wanted and
collected from the Jews, as long as Rome got its share first. That
meant they were extremely wealthy, but they got their wealth
directly from the taxes and personal income they collected from
their fellow Jews. Prostitutes were not hated quite as much, but
they were in the lowest level of Jewish society.

For Jesus to tell these proper Jewish religious leaders that tax
collectors and prostitutes were getting into the kingdom of God
before them would have been so offensive that it's hard to wrap
our minds around.

No wonder they wanted to crucify Jesus soon after that.

Why would he say something like that?

Let's look at Jesus's words to find out.

In the last verse, Jesus says John (the Baptist) came to the Jewish people in righteousness—meaning living a holy life—but they didn't believe him, even though the tax collectors and prostitutes did. He says that even though they saw the tax collectors and prostitutes believing John's message, they (the Jewish religious leaders) still refused. They failed to believe John's message, and now they have their awaited messiah right in front of them, but they still refuse to believe.

Their hearts are hard and they fail to believe.

But the hearts of the despised tax collectors and prostitutes were being transformed and changed, as they believed the message and signs of Jesus.

I think these Jewish religious leaders, like almost all religious leaders, were more worried about doing the right thing and following the rules in front of all their people rather than being open to what Jesus said and did. They had too much vested interest in how things used to be, so they wouldn't even consider the possibility of changing.

This is tragic.

But religious leaders are always in danger of falling into this trap, just as many American Christian leaders fall into the same trap today. Too many of them are stuck in how things operated in the past instead of trying to lead people boldly into the future. They fear the future and long for the past instead of looking to the past for guidance and embracing the future with optimism and hope.

This is also why I say Jesus killed religion.

But human beings brought it back.

Let me explain.

Before Jesus, every religious system on earth, including that of the ancient Jews, was based on a temple where priests served by giving offerings from the people to appease whatever god was represented in the temple. The Jewish people were unique because they were the first people on earth to believe in only one God, since all other people and religions until that day were polytheistic (they believed in many gods); but the basic religious system that God gave the Jews worked in the same way as all the other temple-based religions.

Priests worked as intermediaries by giving offerings to God, and there were certain regulations for where different people in society could go in the temple. This was pretty much how all the ancient religious systems worked. They were dedicated to all the deities of that world, and they all had priests who interceded between the deity and the people by offering gifts at the altar to appease that god.

The religious system God gave the ancient Jews was based on that very common ancient religious system so it was something they would be familiar with and understand. But instead of drawing people to the false gods pagans worshiped all over the ancient world, the God of the Jews wanted his temple to draw people to the one true God, calling people away from all the other false gods and deities.

That system was based on having animal sacrifices that would pay for the sins of the ancient Jews, but this was only temporary in order to point the way to how God was going to deal with our sins once and for all.

When Jesus was crucified as the sinless lamb of God, he laid down the perfect sacrifice on our behalf and fulfilled the Old Testament law for all of us. [34] That meant the presence of God was no longer going to dwell in the temple, but instead in the hearts of his people.

Suddenly, for the first time in history, there was no use for a temple.

There was no use for priests to act as intermediaries.

This is why Christians and followers of Jesus shouldn't follow the ethical and religious commands of the Old Testament; they simply don't apply to us. They applied to ancient Jews living under the old system, but not to followers of Jesus.

This is why the New Testament never mentions priests as part of the community of followers of Jesus.

It mentions pastors, prophets, and things like that, but nowhere does it mention priests.

Why?

Because it's completely inappropriate for priests to be part of our community, since there is no temple for them to work in.

This is how Jesus killed religion, redefining it as a new radical way of life.

He eliminated the need for it.

But, tragically, followers of Jesus couldn't handle the raw presence of God in their lives, and they slowly defaulted back to what they knew before: temple-based religions with priests who act as intermediaries. This is exactly what the Roman Catholic Church did during the 5–10th centuries A.D.

They began treating church buildings as sacred temples.

As if there is anything holy or sacred about a building.

They forgot that the church is the people of God.

Not a building.

They even created a class of priests who are supposed to act as intermediaries for the people, and who work in the churches just like the priests did in temples throughout the ancient world. They forgot that God now dwells, by his spirit, in each believer and we therefore don't need anyone to act as an intermediary between God and us.

That's why the Roman Catholic Church has priests instead of pastors.

That's also one of the main reasons why Martin Luther started the reformation.

He recognized that the Catholic Church had resuscitated and Christianized a dead religious system that was based on temples and priests who act as intermediaries between the people and God. Luther rightly recognized this terrible sequence of events, and eventually led a movement to restore what he saw as the faith and community of the New Testament.

That's why Protestants don't have priests.

We have pastors, prophets, and lots of other things—just like the New Testament community did—but we recognize we are God's temple because he dwells in each of us. That means we don't need priests, because we are all priests who act as intermediaries between God and the non-believing world. This is what the reformers referred to as the *priesthood of all believers*, and it was a foundational part of the protestant reformation.

So, what can we say about all this?

Jesus killed religion.

But, sadly, human beings couldn't handle the direct access to God.

So we brought religion back.

The Roman Catholic Church created a Christianized version of the dead temple and priest religions that dominated the ancient world. This should be a warning for every paid Christian leader out there: God doesn't need you, me, or any of us, and he could probably do a better job of leading if we would get out of his way. [35]

5

FAITH IN ACTION

Time and time again, Jesus places a huge amount of importance on our actions. While what we believe about God is important, I think most American Christians have emphasized that far too much, and failed to give our actions the value and worth that they consistently have in the teachings of Jesus. In fact, many times Jesus even goes so far as to say that our actions will determine whether or not we are his followers—whether or not we are the children of God we claim to be. But, since most American Christians have such a negative view of those same actions, we need Jesus to set the record straight.

The Golden Rule

At one point in the Sermon on the Mount, Jesus unloads this amazing nugget: "*In everything do to others as you would have them do to you; for this is the law and the prophets.*" [36]

During the time of ancient Israel, the ancient Jews had lots of prohibitions about things they couldn't do. In fact, there are over 600 commands in the Jewish scriptures (what Christians call the Old Testament). Around the time of Jesus, famous rabbis would often summarize the writings in different ways. Some said that a faithful Jew shouldn't do anything to anyone that they would not like someone to do to them.

That meant that if they didn't want people to attack or hit them, then they shouldn't attack or hit others. If they didn't want people to deceive or lie to them, then they shouldn't deceive or lie to others. If they didn't want people to steal from them, then they shouldn't steal from others. If they didn't want people to oppress or kill them, then they shouldn't oppress or kill others.

But there's a problem with all this.

All these summaries only talk about what ancient Jews shouldn't do.

They never actually talk about what they should do.

Only Jesus ever summarized the Old Testament by talking about what his followers should do, as he explained in these words. Jesus changed the negative commands of these summaries into a positive command that he wanted his Jewish followers to do from then on.

This was huge because no longer was it enough for ancient Jews to simply not hit, attack, lie, steal, and murder, and think they were fulfilling God's will in their lives. If they wanted to be followers of Jesus, then they had to go beyond that and actually do the things they would like someone to do to them. And, amazingly, Jesus says this one proactive command summarizes all the ethical commands of the Jewish scriptures.

This means that for every follower of Jesus, if we want people to love us and show us compassion, we must love them and show them compassion.

If we want people to forgive us, then we must forgive them.

If we want people to treat us honestly and fairly, then we must treat them honestly and fairly.

If we want people to help and support us, then we must help and support them.

If we want people to trust and believe us, then we must trust and believe them.

If we want people to care for us, then we must care for them.

If we want people to respect us, then we must respect them.

If we want people to admire and appreciate us, then we must admire and appreciate them.

This one short saying of Jesus is loaded with every kind of ethical action and command included in it. Perhaps nowhere does Jesus say so much with so little, because this tiny saying is one of the most revolutionary things he ever says. It literally includes everything we do and the way we treat everyone we come across.

This should also rule out the violent ethics of the millions of American Christians who support and participate in violence and warfare, because if they attack or kill people, then they are clearly not treating those people how they would like to be treated (unless they have a death-wish and want to be killed).

There is no way around this. If you are one of the American Christians who supports violence and warfare of any kind, then you need to know that your actions contradict the words of the man you call your lord and master.

You are clearly not treating the people you attack and kill as you would like to be treated, unless you want to die, so you are failing to live out these words.

In fact, you're doing the exact opposite of what Jesus wanted us to do when he said these words.

If you don't follow the words of Jesus on this issue, then he is clearly not your lord or master. You are bowing down to the idol of whatever is making you attack and kill the same people Jesus calls us to love and pray for. Whether it's fear, hatred, American nationalism, ignorance, or anything else, all those things will call us to attack people, but Jesus shows yet again why no follower of Jesus who takes their faith in him seriously should ever attack or kill anyone.

Because attacking and killing people isn't doing to them what we would like done to us.

In fact, it's as far from that as anyone can get.

The Greatest Commandment

A scribe came to Jesus to ask him a question:

> One of the scribes came near and heard them disputing with one another, and seeing that he answered them well, he asked him, "Which commandment is the first of all?" Jesus answered, "The first is, 'Hear, O Israel: the Lord our God, the Lord is one; you shall love the Lord your God with all your heart, and with all your soul, and with

all your mind, and with all your strength.' The second is this, 'You shall love your neighbor as yourself.' There is no other commandment greater than these." Then the scribe said to him, "You are right, Teacher; you have truly said that 'he is one, and besides him there is no other'; and 'to love him with all the heart, and with all the understanding, and with all the strength,' and 'to love one's neighbor as oneself,'—this is much more important than all whole burnt offerings and sacrifices." When Jesus saw that he answered wisely, he said to him, "You are not far from the kingdom of God." [37]

This is fascinating! A scribe asks Jesus which commandment of the more than 600 commandments in the Jewish scriptures is the most important. Jesus responds by quoting the *shema*, which was a Jewish statement of belief taken right out of scripture. [38]

It says God is one. This was important since all other peoples and religions at that time were polytheistic.

Jesus says the second most important is that *you shall love your neighbor as yourself,* and says all the Jewish scriptures hang on those two.

While this is true, I want to address something about loving neighbors. Jews at that time thought they could be faithful Jews by loving God and loving their neighbor as themselves, as this passage mentions. But a problem arose: Jews loved their Jewish neighbors, but hated and despised non-Jewish people and nations. They called them gentiles, and thought of them as almost sub-human.

Jews during the time of Jesus thought it was okay for them to love God and their Jewish neighbors, but then despise everyone else. So they hated non-Jews. They had inherited about 1,400 years of hatred towards nations like Egypt, Assyria, Babylon, Greece, and Rome. The Jewish people at the time of Jesus thought it was their duty to hate and despise those people and nations, but Jesus would not accept that hatred and animosity from his followers.

That's why he calls his followers, including you and me, to love and pray for our enemies. [39]

Jesus will not allow his followers to love only God, our neighbors, and friends, as the Jews of his day were doing.

Jesus calls his followers to extend our love even to our enemies.

And anyone who claims the name of Christ, but doesn't do that, is not following the words of Jesus.

Anyone who claims the name of Christ, but supports violence or actions taken against even our enemies, is not following Jesus.

Love One Another as I Have Loved You

Just a few hours before Jesus was arrested, he spent his last night with his disciples and told them the most important things they needed to know when he was gone. Jesus began his last few hours by washing their feet, and then said this:

> *I give you a new commandment, that you love one another. Just as I have loved you, you also should love one another. By this everyone will know that you are my disciples, if you have love for one another.* [40]

Jesus tells his followers they must love one another, but not in some non-specific emotional way that most American Christians think he's talking about. Instead, Jesus tells them exactly how he wants and expects them to love one another: in the same way he has loved them. Jesus spent three years loving these men by serving and teaching them, putting their needs and growth ahead of his own, and now he tells them they are to love one another in the same way when he's gone.

On top of that, Jesus just performed the duty of a slave as he washed the feet of all his disciples, and now that he's finished, he tells them they are to love one another in the same way: by humbling and denying themselves to serve one another.

Jesus is literally calling them to love one another with the same selfless, reckless, and abandoned love he loves them with, but not in some non-specific emotional sense that most Christians turn this love into. Jesus tells them very specifically that their love and treatment of one another is to be based on his love and treatment of them.

Why is this so important?

We see why in the last line. Jesus says that everyone else— meaning the people who aren't part of the community of Jesus— will know his followers if we love one another in this way. This is huge.

Those of us who know these stories know Jesus will be executed very soon after this interaction, and that he even dies on behalf of his people. He dies to defeat sin and death—and set his followers free from them. He literally lays down his life in loving sacrifice for everyone who will come to him. If Jesus lived and died as a loving sacrifice, then how much more should we who claim to follow him do the same?

If this is true, then why are there so few Christians who are ready and willing to follow Jesus on the road of living as a loving sacrifice?

Why do most of them only think about Jesus giving them more of what they already have: things like money, success, fame, and recognition? While far too many followers of Jesus seem to only want those things, that's not what Jesus calls us to pursue. Jesus calls us to love and serve our world with the same self-sacrificial love and service he demonstrated and taught.

If all this is true, then how is it that the vast majority of American Christians don't treat one another with the same love Jesus did?

How is it that most of them set out to attack, criticize, condemn, judge, destroy, and even kill other Christians and followers of Jesus when they view them as threats?

How is it that they support, and participate in, violent wars and actions both at home and abroad, where Christians are persecuting, destroying, and killing other Christians who happen to disagree with them or who simply live in a different country?

These kinds of so-called Christians have forgotten who their lord and master is.

They have completely severed themselves from the teachings of Jesus and the New Testament.

They have stopped following Jesus.

I wish those violent people would stop claiming the name of Christ altogether, because their violent hypocrisy and actions contradict the teaching of Jesus and are causing non-Christians to want nothing to do with him.

This is part of the reason that followers of Jesus, for the first 300 years of Church history, refused to partake in any violence. To them, that would have been like denying their lord and master, Jesus, who called them to act and respond with the same self-sacrificial love he taught and displayed.

The Roman Empire often executed them for their faithfulness to Jesus and their refusal to bow down and serve Rome, but they were more than willing to lay down their lives for the one who laid down his life for them.

They simply refused to compromise on that issue.

All this changed drastically, however, in 313 A.D. when the emperor Constantine legalized Christianity. Then his son declared it the official religion of the Roman Empire, which meant for the first time ever, it was illegal *not* to be a Christian in the Roman Empire. Suddenly, millions of Roman pagans were forced to convert to Christianity or suffer the wrath of Rome's armies, which all went out persecuting and killing any who refused to convert to the new official religion of the empire. [41]

This was the first time in human history that violence was ever associated with Christianity.

But, tragically, it would not be the last.

Instead, pretty much all the countries in Europe soon copied the basic model of the Roman Empire and the Roman Catholic Church, and forced people in those areas to convert or die.

Their militaries went out waging wars against non-Christians, as well as fellow brothers and sisters in the faith who happened to live in a different country. They all thought they were being faithful to the teachings and will of Jesus.

In fact, this horrific behavior reached its peak in the Inquisition, which was an official program of extreme punishment, torture, and execution that the Roman Catholic Church ran with the governments of Italy, France, and Spain. Its goal was to rid their citizens of any thoughts or writings that could be deemed non-Christian, and thus heretical. [42]

Scientists were only allowed to publish things that agreed with the official teaching of the Roman Catholic Church; and the same can be said for authors, many of whom found themselves black-listed, which meant the Roman Catholic Church banned their works because they were not deemed to be Christian enough.

The Inquisition systematically hunted, persecuted, tortured, and killed hundreds of thousands, potentially even millions, of people. Anyone who was accused of not being a Christian was tortured in an effort to elicit a confession and conversion, as they had to profess their faith in Jesus and in the Holy Roman Catholic Church.

If they didn't, then their torture would end in execution.

By drowning.

Being burned alive.

And all kinds of other horrific ways of dying.

In fact, hundreds of thousands of women were burned alive because they were accused of being witches or non-Christians. This is why Dr. Gregory Boyd says, *"The church . . . had become a horde of savage warlords."* [43]

These kinds of evil actions may seem too horrible to imagine, but American Christian soldiers essentially do the same thing when they think they are serving God's will by persecuting, destroying, and killing the very same people Jesus calls us to love and pray for. Jesus said the love between his followers should let other people know we are his people, but these self-proclaiming Christians hate, destroy, and kill the very same followers of Jesus we're called to model the love of Jesus with.

It's time to wake up.

It's time to open our eyes.

If you are a Christian who supports or participates in this kind of violence, I have a few questions for you:

Where can you find even one verse in the New Testament that justifies your violence and killing?

Where do you base your violent ethics?

I know it's not Jesus or the New Testament, because not one of those verses can be used to justify violence, and anytime followers of Jesus base our ethics on anything that's not Jesus (or at least the New Testament) we run into serious problems. The Old Testament is great for understanding the story of God's working in the world, but we can't go there to base our ethics.

It was written for ancient Jews who lived in a completely different culture, time, and place, and who related to God in a very different way than modern Christians do. [44] When Christians go to the Old Testament for our ethics, we end up doing this kind of horrific stuff in the name of Jesus.

And for that, we must repent.

We must also return to the radical, non-violent enemy-love of Jesus and the first 300 years of church history. Only then will we be able to heal and get back on the correct path after 1700 years of following the path of violence and destruction. [45]

So how about you?

Do you love your brothers and sisters in the faith, like Jesus did, or do you attack and condemn them if they threaten you or think differently?

Do you love and pray for your enemies, like Jesus did, or do you hate and attack them?

Do Not Judge

Later in the Sermon on the Mount, Jesus says this about judging people:

> *Do not judge, so that you may not be judged. For with the judgment you make you will be judged, and the measure you give will be the measure you get. Why do you see the speck in your neighbor's eye, but do not notice the log in your own eye? Or how can you say to your neighbor, "Let me take the speck out of your eye," while the log is in your own eye? You hypocrite, first take the log out of your own eye, and then you will see clearly to take the speck out of your neighbor's eye.* [46]

When I was in college, there was a group of right wing pro-life Christians that would show up each school year, set up massive 15-foot-high posters of aborted fetuses, and then preach a message of condemnation and judgment to the tens of thousands of people on campus.

This group set up on a huge lawn and then preached a message that was nothing but judgment and condemnation. Every time they showed up, I almost got sick to my stomach because I thought this was what the thousands of students and faculty were going to think Christianity was. This group was so full of judgment and condemnation that I learned the best thing for me to do was to avoid them altogether.

Now, even if you are pro-life, as I am, we have no right to judge and condemn people like this.

Jesus is very clear that he is the judge of human beings, not us.

In this passage, he tells us not to judge others at all unless we want to be judged with the same scale we use to judge. Because of this, I think the right-wing pro-lifers at my school will be in for a big surprise when they die and find themselves face to face with Jesus. But I will not go further than that about the state of their salvation, because Jesus says that's his concern, not mine.

In fact, the only thing followers of Jesus are supposed to do when we face that kind of judgment and criticism is respond with love.

We are to love everyone, even if they attack, condemn, or judge us, because that's how God is. God loves everyone, including the people who hate or deny him, so if we claim to be children of God, then we are called by our heavenly father into the family business of loving everyone; and that includes loving the people who hate and try to harm us.

One of my friends once told me that when he took this command seriously, it lightened his load and gave him a true sense of joy. He said that he had incorrectly assumed it was the unstated job and responsibility of Christians to figure out why people do bad things, and to assign blame for them. But this passage freed him from the burden of thinking he had to judge everyone, which let him accept and love people as they were and experience deep joy in that process.

This is the kind of revolutionary grace I hope we all experience when we take these words of Jesus seriously. My friend discovered a source of true joy in these words that he had never experienced before, and my hope is that we can all tap into the same thing.

My hope is that we can all discover the freedom and joy of being able to love everyone exactly how they are, without trying to assign guilt or blame for the things they do.

My hope is that we'll have the courage to set aside our judging and criticism, and instead follow in my friend's grace-filled footsteps.

After all, that's what grace is.

And that's how God loves us.

The Wise and Foolish Builders

Jesus finishes the Sermon on the Mount with these fascinating words:

> *Everyone then who hears these words of mine and acts on them will be like a wise man who built his house on rock. The rain fell, the*

floods came, and the winds blew and beat on that house, but it did not fall, because it had been founded on rock. And everyone who hears these words of mine and does not act on them will be like a foolish man who built his house on sand. The rain fell, and the floods came, and the winds blew and beat against that house, and it fell—and great was its fall! [47]

According to this story, the only difference between the wise man and the fool is that the wise man hears the words of Jesus and does them, but the fool hears the words of Jesus and doesn't do them. Both men have the words and teachings of Jesus, but only one does them, and that's why he's wise. The fool refuses to do what Jesus commands him, even though he knows exactly what Jesus calls and expects him to do.

I would say Christians who participate in violence, vengeance, revenge, retaliation, or attacks on anyone fall into the same category as this fool.

They have the teachings and commands of Jesus, but they refuse to put them into practice. Here, Jesus is talking about what we do, not what we believe about him or God, and that alone is what determines whether we align ourselves with the wise man or with the fool.

For example, do we refuse to retaliate when people attack or hurt us, or do we try to get even?

Do we respond to evil by returning the same evil back, or by loving them?

Do we seek healing and restoration, or revenge?

Do we participate in, or support, violence and destruction?

Do we love and pray for our enemies, or do we hate them and try to eliminate them?

If we read, teach, recite, and memorize the ethical teachings and commands of Jesus, but we don't actually do them, then we truly are the fools. I hope we can all see how serious Jesus is about the people who do this; he says those who do this are building their lives and faith on a foundation that will lead to destruction.

That means that if you claim the name of Jesus, and still support or participate in violence or war, you're not doing what Jesus told you to do. That means you're now in the same status as the fool in this analogy, and you need to know that, no matter what you personally think about these issues, these words of Jesus reveal the truth of who you are. You are playing the part of the fool.

You are reading the words of Jesus about loving our enemies and refusing to use violence or revenge, but you're not putting them into action.

And that means that, according to the analogy Jesus uses here, you are the fool.

That also means you are building your life and faith on a foundation that will lead to destruction.

If this applies to you, the good news is there is still time to change.

But you need to repent.

You need to stop doing or supporting violence, ask Jesus for forgiveness, and then commit yourself to following his teachings about living with the same non-violent, self-sacrificial enemy-love that Jesus taught and demonstrated. According to Jesus, the only way his followers should be treating our enemies is by loving them and praying for them, and anything beyond that means we're not the children of God we think we are. [48]

That may sound harsh, but those aren't my words.

They are the words of Jesus.

The question is whether or not you choose to follow them.

6

THE GREAT COMMISSION

Most Christians think of the Great Commission at the end of Matthew's Gospel when they think about Jesus sending out his disciples. While that is an important text for understanding how Jesus sends us out, it is certainly not the only text that deals with that issue. In fact, there are many of them, and as we will see in this chapter, these words once again challenge much of what we think about Jesus sending us into the world. They force us to rethink our small ideas, and they encourage us to default to the radical words of Jesus.

As the Father Has Sent Me, I Am Sending You

Most of us think of the Great Commission in Matthew's Gospel as the quintessential passage about Jesus sending out his disciples to continue his ministry. But I like this lesser-known version from John's Gospel even better. It's simple but profound. Here are Jesus's words to his disciples as he is about to return to the presence of his Father and commission his disciples to continue his work and ministry:

> Jesus said to them again, "Peace be with you. As the Father has sent me, so I send you." When he had said this, he breathed on them and said to them, "Receive the Holy Spirit." [49]

Jesus appears to his disciples and says to them, *as the Father has sent me, so I send you.* This is incredible! Jesus is sending out his disciples in the same way the Father sent Jesus. How did the Father send Jesus? In the power of the Holy Spirit, which is why he breathes on them and has them receive the same spirit that came over him when he was baptized.

The Father also sent him out proclaiming the good news of the kingdom of God, in self-sacrificial love, to save the world and not condemn it, to heal, to restore, to redeem, to confront and destroy evil, to set people free, and to humbly serve a broken world. If this describes the way God the Father sent out Jesus, and if Jesus now sends his followers out in the same way, then that means we are sent in all these ways, too.

We are sent to proclaim the good news of the kingdom of God.

We are sent in self-sacrificial love.

We are sent to save the world and not to condemn it.

We are sent to heal.

We are sent to restore.

We are sent to redeem.

We are sent to confront evil and destroy it.

We are sent to set people free.

We are sent to humbly serve a broken world.

None of these things are easy, but this is what Jesus calls us to. We are called to follow him and his ways, and there is no better way to do this than by going into the world and living our lives in the same way he did.

This won't be easy, but nothing about following Jesus is.

And we'll find joy, fulfillment, purpose, and meaning in the struggle.

We Will Do Greater Things Than Jesus

Jesus says that his followers will do even greater things than he did:

> Very truly, I tell you, the one who believes in me will also do the works that I do and, in fact, will do greater works than these, because I am going to the Father. [50]

This is shocking, and used to leave me baffled, because Jesus extended his invitation to absolutely everyone he came across. He treated women with a respect and dignity that no one in the ancient world could even come close to. He did the same thing with notorious sinners like tax collectors and prostitutes. Jesus also healed all kinds of people from all kinds of conditions and illnesses. He even raised someone from the dead, for crying out loud!

So, when I used to read this, I asked myself: how can I do more than what Jesus has already done?

I can't.

And I'm right; I can't do it alone.

But Jesus is addressing all his disciples and I think he means this as a corporate statement about what his present and future followers will do, and in that way we will do more than him because we're more than one person.

Jesus probably healed a few hundred people—maybe a few thousand at the most. But the billions of followers of Jesus throughout history will heal way more than that. In the same way, Jesus offered the invitation to follow him to everyone he came in contact with. But, again, that couldn't have been more than a few thousand to a few hundred thousand people.

Yet billions of followers of Jesus can extend that invitation to billions of people.

To every single human being alive.

When Jesus returned to the Father after his resurrection, he instantly became way more powerful than he was while he was on earth as the person of Jesus. Because as Jesus, he was present in only one person: himself. In Jesus, his spirit was present only in himself. It wasn't available to other people, including even his disciples at that time.

But after Jesus returned to the Father, he sent his own spirit to live in his followers, so he could lead and guide us in ways he never could before.

That means the potential for Jesus in the billions who claim his name is far greater than it ever was when he was only present in his own body and life. Now Jesus walks with us. In fact, as he has said, he will never leave us or forsake us.

So, in light of all this, it makes perfect sense that Jesus would say we will do greater things than him. This is true because of the sheer number of people he can now accompany and work through, which he couldn't do when he was present only in the person of Jesus. Now that every follower of Jesus has the spirit of Jesus—the Holy Spirit—living in us, there is literally no limit to what he can do or accomplish through us.

Feed My Lambs

This is one of my favorite interactions of Jesus anywhere, but I need to set the scene so we understand what's going on. Jesus has been crucified, and this is the last time he appeared to his disciples after his resurrection and before he ascended back to the Father. Many of Jesus's disciples aren't sure about what to do now that he's gone, so they go back to what they did before they met Jesus: fishing.

Peter and others go out and don't catch anything. Then the resurrected Jesus shows up at daybreak on the beach, but the disciples don't know it's him. He asks if they caught any fish and they say no. So he tells them to throw their net on the other side and they do, and they catch so many fish that they can't haul in the net.

This was the exact way Jesus called them the first time he called them. Suddenly, Peter realizes it's Jesus on the beach, so he jumps naked into the water and swims as fast as he can to him. The other disciples drag the net and come in the boat, since they weren't far from land.

When they get to the beach, they see a fire with Jesus sitting there cooking fish and bread. All of them know it is Jesus; they don't need to ask him. Jesus feeds them with bread and fish as they eat breakfast together again. Then, the story picks up here:

> *When they had finished breakfast, Jesus said to Simon Peter, "Simon son of John, do you love me more than these?" He said to him, "Yes, Lord; you know that I love you." Jesus said to him, "Feed my lambs." A second time he said to him, "Simon son of John, do you love me?" He said to him, "Yes, Lord; you know that I love you." Jesus said to him, "Tend my sheep." He said to him the third time, "Simon son of John, do you love me?" Peter felt hurt because he said to him the third time, "Do you love me?" And he said to him, "Lord, you know everything; you know that I love you." Jesus said to him, "Feed my sheep. Very truly, I tell you, when you were younger, you used to fasten your own belt and to go wherever you wished. But when you grow old, you will stretch out your hands, and someone else will fasten a belt around you and take you where you do not wish to go." (He said this to indicate the kind of death by which he would glorify God.) After this he said to him, "Follow me."* [51]

What Jesus does with Peter here is absolutely stunning. We must remember that, earlier, Peter said he would be faithful to Jesus until death, even if all the other disciples abandoned him. He promised to be faithful no matter what. But then Peter famously denied ever knowing Jesus three times, only a few hours after Jesus had been arrested.

Probably no one among the disciples is feeling lower than Peter at this point. Three times he denied knowing Jesus. He was within earshot of Jesus, who even looked at him after the third one to make sure Peter knew that Jesus knew what Peter had done.

At this point, Peter must be thinking he is the lowest of the low. But Jesus doesn't. Jesus restores Peter by asking him if Peter loves him exactly three times, one for every time Peter denied him. But not only that, Jesus gives Peter his ultimate calling into ministry by asking him to feed the lambs and sheep of Jesus.

How can Jesus do that?

How can he overlook Peter's pride, arrogance, and faithlessness and call him into the single most important position of the community of Jesus as they move forward?

He doesn't do it because Peter is perfect. In fact, it's for the exact opposite reason. Peter finally realizes how imperfect he is. Peter was always the one disciple who thought he was far more faithful, bold, courageous, and strong than he really was. In fact, he almost flaunted it at times, and was often rebuked by Jesus because of it.

Now, finally, Peter knows exactly how weak he is, in and of himself.

He knows exactly how cowardly he is apart from Jesus.

He knows exactly how dependent, fragile, prideful, arrogant, and faithless he is.

And it's not in spite of these things, but because of them, that Jesus gives him his highest call into ministry.

Because Peter is going to lead the community of followers of Jesus from here on out, and he's going to need to help people recover when they think they can do things in their own strength, but can't. He will need to help people pick up the pieces when they get puffed up with pride, and then fail; when they say they'll be faithful, but aren't; and when they think they will be bold and courageous, but can't.

He'll know exactly how they feel because he went through the same thing.

I love this because Jesus doesn't use Peter because Peter is perfect.

He uses Peter because Peter finally realizes how imperfect he is.

And that's when we become truly useful in the hands of Jesus.

This is one of my favorite things about Jesus: he uses imperfect and lowly people like you and me to change the world.

He invites us into his revolution, and it's not for the faint of heart.

His revolution isn't one of violence or destruction.

It's a revolution of self-sacrificial love.

And he wants you and me to help him lead the charge.

Go Make Followers

The last words of Jesus in the Gospel of Matthew are what we call the Great Commission, because it includes Jesus commissioning his disciples to go into the world and teach them everything Jesus taught them:

All authority in heaven and on earth has been given to me. Go therefore and make disciples of all nations, baptizing them in the name of the Father and of the Son and of the Holy Spirit, and teaching them to obey everything that I have commanded you. And remember, I am with you always, to the end of the age. [52]

There are a couple things I want to mention about this. To begin with: Jesus calls his followers to *make disciples of all nations.* Disciples are students who learn from a master teacher, just like Luke was the disciple of Yoda in the original Star Wars trilogy. Disciples follow around their master teacher and learn by following their teacher in on-the-job-training.

So a disciple is a follower.

And a disciple of Jesus is a follower of Jesus.

That's why I don't refer to myself as a *Christian,* and instead call myself a *follower of Jesus.*

This is also the only way Jesus refers to the community of people who follow him. But if we don't actually follow the teachings of Jesus, then it doesn't matter if we call ourselves Christians or anything else. When we fail to follow the teachings of Jesus, we fail to follow Jesus. When that happens, we fail to be followers of Jesus.

We fail to be Christians.

For example, when we follow the ways of violence, destruction, and death, we stop following Jesus.

When we support or participate in wars, we stop following Jesus.

When we follow the ways of revenge and retaliation, we stop following Jesus.

When we try to attack, destroy, or kill our enemies, we stop following Jesus.

When we put ourselves first, we stop following Jesus.

To the extent that we do this, we need to repent and return to Jesus. We need to ask God to teach us how to live out the self-sacrificial enemy-love of Jesus, and to let Jesus replace our hidden agendas with his agenda. Only then will we be able to participate with him in fulfilling this great commission, and only then will we be able to make disciples of Jesus in each and every nation.

I am convinced we can't make followers of Jesus if we aren't already following him ourselves.

How can you give more of your life over to him?

7

NOT AN EASY PATH

Unfortunately, many Christians try to make it easier for non-Christians to place their trust in Jesus by only emphasizing the good things he can do for us. Now, there are lots of amazing things he can do in us, so I don't want to discount that; but these Christians deceive people by overlooking the fact that following Jesus also means taking on a whole new set of challenges. Jesus, ever the contrarian, never minced his words about how hard it would be to follow him.

The Narrow and Broad Gate and Road

In the Sermon on the Mount, Jesus says this:

> *Enter through the narrow gate; for the gate is wide and the road is easy that leads to destruction, and there are many who take it. For the gate is narrow and the road is hard that leads to life, and there are few who find it.* [53]

Jesus is giving us a warning with these words. He says there's a gate and road that are wide and easy to travel. Because of this, there are many people on it. The gate and road Jesus is referring to are the ones that everyone who rejects Jesus is traveling. It's easy because those people can do whatever they want, whenever they want, since they can be loyal to whichever higher power or purpose they feel like; or they can reject all of them.

When Jesus says there are many people on the road that leads to destruction, I think he's severely underestimating the numbers. I would argue that most of our world probably fits into this group. We're talking about hundreds of millions of people, if not billions. This road is easy because the people who travel on it can do whatever they want, but it leads to (eternal) destruction.

I know this road because I lived on it for years until I came to Jesus in my 20's.

It's so easy to walk down, but, like Jesus says, it leads to destruction.

On the other hand, Jesus says the gate and road that lead to (eternal) life are narrow ones, with few people traveling them. This road is hard to travel, but it's the only one that leads us to true and eternal life.

Why is it hard to travel?

Because we must listen and live by the words of Jesus, who is our master and lord, while the people on the other road can do whatever they want.

Those of us who travel on this road must learn to humble ourselves and put others first.

We must learn to serve others instead of being served.

We must learn to trust in God's strength instead of our own.

We must refuse and reject violence and retaliation, while the other road lives by them.

We must learn to forgive instead of getting even.

So what does all this mean?

It means our job is to get as many people to transfer from the road that leads to destruction to the road that leads to life. How do we do that? By having them commit their lives to Jesus; by following his words and teachings. We all must recognize that he is our lord and master.

Taking Up Our Cross to Follow Jesus

Jesus spoke these heavy words to a crowd:

> If any want to become my followers, let them deny themselves and take up their cross and follow me. For those who want to save their life will lose it, and those who lose their life for my sake, and for the sake of the gospel, will save it. For what will it profit them to gain the whole world and forfeit their life? [54]

What does Jesus mean by take up our crosses? He is pre-shadowing the kind of death he will suffer at the hands of the Romans. Crucifixion was invented by them to be the most painful, agonizing, and humiliating way to die. It was so brutal that Roman citizens were exempt from it, and they never brought it up in polite company.

It was so horrific that Romans had to invent a new word to describe it.

Nothing in their vocabulary could describe how grotesque and painful it was.

We still see the Latin root of that word in our English word *excruciating*.

Which comes from the Latin root *ex-crux*, and means *from the cross* in Latin.

Crucifixion was the most painful and horrific mode of execution human beings had come up with at that point, and, amazingly, this is exactly what Jesus is referring to when he says we must pick up our crosses if we want to follow him. Jesus is saying that if we want to follow him, we must be ready to deny ourselves and kill the person we used to be.

He's saying that we must go through a certain kind of death, where we put to death our old self. We let Jesus kill it. Then, after that, Jesus will give us a new self, a new life, and a new will to live for; and our life will be much more filled with purpose, joy, and meaning than it ever was before.

But the only way to get to that point is through death.

We must die.

We must put to death our old self, mind, heart, and will.

And then Jesus will give us new ones.

This isn't easy, but that's what Jesus calls us to.

People Who Leave Family Will Get More

One time, Peter lamented to Jesus that the disciples had left everything to follow him, and Jesus answered with these words:

> *Truly I tell you, there is no one who has left house or brothers or sisters or mother or father or children or fields, for my sake and for the sake of the good news, who will not receive a hundredfold now in this age—houses, brothers and sisters, mothers and children, and fields, with persecutions—and in the age to come eternal life.* [55]

Our motivation for following and serving Jesus should be based on things like love, gratitude, and appreciation. That means we serve him because we love and appreciate him. We want to serve him. That also means we may find ourselves in difficult situations, or having to leave people behind to fulfill what Jesus calls us to. We are supposed to do that because we want to; not because we feel obligated.

Likewise, we follow Jesus now to make a difference in this world, not primarily so we will have eternal life when we die; but these words of Jesus make it clear that we will receive a great reward in the life to come if we endure hardship or suffering now.

Jesus assures us that whatever we have left to follow him will be given back to us in the age to come, and that we will receive much more than we had in this life. We may be asked to leave behind our families or friends to follow Jesus into some unknown place, and we may even be killed in the process; but Jesus reassures us that we will be more than paid with a reward in the age to come when he establishes his kingdom on earth forever.

This is encouraging for those of us who sacrifice much for the call to follow Jesus, and it should give us peace because we know that even if we die serving Jesus, we will be greatly rewarded. This should help us deny ourselves and follow him wherever he leads us. We can be confident that any pain and suffering we go through now, for his sake, will be worth it when he returns to establish his kingdom.

I know these kinds of words definitely comforted me during my years in Latin America, doing long-term ministry and missions.

They weren't the reason I went, but they did reassure me that, even though I was leaving behind all my friends, family, culture, and country, I knew that I would receive more in the age to come because of it. I knew my sacrifice and service wouldn't go in vain, and that even if I died in the process, my reward would be great.

We should never do things just so we can have a reward, but it is good to know that those of us who set out to follow Jesus into difficult situations will be compensated. While our actions may escape the public eye, they never escape God's eyes. He sees everything we do and will reward us accordingly.

Followers Must Hate Their Families and Carry Crosses

Jesus doesn't want us to hate our family members, but you wouldn't think that from these words:

> Whoever comes to me and does not hate father and mother, wife and children, brothers and sisters, yes, and even life itself, cannot be my disciple. [56]

While it seems like Jesus wants us to hate our family members, he doesn't. Jesus is making one of the most radical statements he makes anywhere, but he's not saying we need to hate our families. He's saying that anyone who comes to him, and loves their family members more than they love Jesus, isn't worthy of being his disciple.

He's saying that the greater love we have for him should be so much greater than the smaller love we have for our family members that when we compare the two, the smaller love for our family looks almost like hatred.

These are challenging and difficult words, but Jesus meant them.

If we choose our family over him, then we're not worthy of being his disciple.

If we choose our spouses and children before Jesus, then we're not worthy of being his disciple.

We see proof of this interpretation in the fact that Jesus treated his mom with overflowing love when he was on the cross, and told the beloved disciple to take care of his mother when he was dead. [57] Jesus wanted to know that his closest friend was going to take care of his mom, so Jesus took extra care to make arrangements for her because of his love for her, not because he hated her.

And, although Jesus loved his mom, there was nothing she could have said or done that would have caused him to turn from the love, will, and calling his heavenly Father gave him. If she would have called him to do something like that, you can be assured that Jesus would have remained faithful to his heavenly Father first and foremost.

Jesus isn't saying that he wants us to literally hate our family members, but he is implying that if we love our family members more than we love him, then we can't be his disciple.

That's tough.

But he means it.

And many Christians are probably very aware of this tension already. If our families call us to do something that compromises the ethical commands and teachings of Jesus, then we are to side with Jesus. To do anything else is to love them more than we love him. As Jesus himself says, if we do that, then we can't be his disciple.

How can you show your love for your family while still maintaining a greater love and faithfulness to Jesus?

People Will Hate You for Following Jesus

At one point, Jesus is talking to his disciples and says, *"You will be hated by all because of my name."* [58] Jesus is painting the realistic picture of just how many people will be against him and his movement. He paints no false illusions or ideas about how hard it is to follow him.

People will hate us for it.

Lots of them.

In fact, so many will hate us that it will seem like everyone.

But we are always to respond to the hatred of others with the same love and compassion Jesus showed to the world that hated and rejected him. In fact, Jesus loved and prayed for the enemies that hated him, as is seen when he prayed that his Father would forgive the very people who crucified him. [59]

That means we know two things for sure about this. First: we should expect people to hate us because of Jesus. Second: we are still called to never respond to their evil and hatred with evil and hatred, but are instead to love and pray for them. [60] We are to refuse to retaliate or try to get even with them. [61] Instead, we are called to forgive without end, and seek to be reconciled with them. [62]

This may sound crazy.

But that's the only option Jesus gives us.

To take up violence, or to seek revenge or retaliation in any way, is to contradict the crystal-clear teachings of Jesus on these matters. I hope it's clear that so-called Christians who do this have stopped following the teachings of Jesus, and have therefore stopped following Jesus.

The people who do this are following something else, and it's clearly not the words, teachings, and commands of Jesus, the one they say is their lord and master. If they were truly following the words and commands of Jesus, then there is no way they would attack and try to kill the same people Jesus calls us to love, pray for, forgive, and be reconciled with.

But, as Jesus often says, the world will know his true followers not by what we say, but by our fruits and actions. [63]

I couldn't agree more.

III

THE SOCIAL RADICAL

8
_____

HUMILITY

Before Jesus, being called *humble* was an insult. It wasn't something anyone wanted, and it meant the person associated with it was weak and powerless. The ancient world valued the exact opposite values: power and strength. We still see the old meaning when we talk about humble beginnings. That means someone grew up in weakness and poverty, without things like power or strength. Rulers of antiquity would probably have had someone killed if that person insulted them by saying they were humble. And so in Jesus we see something humanity has never seen: the humble king—the humble God! In this chapter, we will see how Jesus, the humble God and king, transformed humility into something to be celebrated.

The Last Will Be First, and the First Will Be Last

Some of the most astonishing, shocking, and unexpected words of Jesus are the exact opposite of what most of us would expect to hear or read, because they normally contradict the way most of our world operates. In fact, on pretty much every page of the four Gospels, which tell us about the life and ministry of Jesus, he says at least one thing that completely overrules or overturns most of the systems and cycles our world lives by. [64]

For example, Jesus says that many people who are first will be last, and many who are last will be first. [65] This is astonishing when we stop to think about it. Jesus is saying that many of the people who are considered last in our culture and world will be considered first when his kingdom is established forever on the earth. He is also saying that many of the people who are first in our world and culture will be last when he establishes his kingdom.

That means those of us who commit ourselves to his teaching by following and serving him will often be laughed at, ridiculed, overlooked, attacked, insulted, or abused; after all, that's part of what it means to be considered the last, or least, in our world. But, according to these words of Jesus, although we will find ourselves in these situations because we are following and serving him, our reward will be great, and we will be vindicated in the future.

These words are meant to reassure and encourage followers of Jesus, because following Jesus isn't easy. It's a life filled with purpose and meaning, but it isn't easy and Jesus never said it would be. In fact, he often warns his followers to count the cost of following him before we do.

After all, it's not easy to put others first.

But that's what Jesus calls us to do.

It's not easy to respond to hatred with love and forgiveness.

But that's what Jesus calls us to do.

It's not easy to respond to attacks with non-violence or seek restoration instead of seeking revenge.

But that's what Jesus calls us to do.

None of these are easy.

But this is what it means to be the last and least.

And if we dare to do that, then we should be encouraged to know that our service will not go in vain. We will receive our reward, but it might not come in this life. That's the point Jesus is making with this unexpected paradox.

He's also warning all the people who are among the first in our world. I'm talking about leaders and people who are powerful, wealthy, arrogant, prideful, selfish, and self-seeking. This is a warning to the people who put themselves first and almost never try to help or care for others.

The warning of this paradox is: *Beware! It may look like you're winning and getting all the recognition now, but, in the end, you will see that the road you chose leads to nothing!*

The example I always think of when I think of the last being first is my younger brother, Jonathan. Jono was born severely mentally and physically disabled, so much so that he was never able to do anything on his own.

He was never able to say one word, take one step, feed himself, or use his body or mind past the control of a 6-10 month baby, even though he lived for 21 years. In fact, when I was younger, I was so angry at God for having a family member like Jono that I turned

my back on God and wanted nothing to do with him for about
10 years.

I didn't come to faith until I was in my 20's, and a large part of
that had to do with my anger about Jono. After years of partying
really hard to forget about God, wanting to just have fun and
enjoy life, I was forced to deal with how empty and meaningless
my life had become. Later, when I started going to church and
making my way back to God, these words from Jesus helped me
interpret Jono's life in a new way.

I knew no one was smaller or less than Jono, because he was as
helpless and dependent as anyone can possibly be. It's simply
impossible to be more dependent and helpless than he was, yet
God had used him powerfully and painfully in the life of me and
my family. God brought lots of really good things out of our experience with Jono, and, eventually, these words from Jesus helped
me see Jono's life differently. They helped me see it, not as the
tragic life I had always viewed it as, but as a staging ground for
the greatness of his future glory.

I knew that if God was real, and if these words of Jesus were true,
then Jono would be first in God's kingdom, because he was the
very last in our world.

I also knew that, if that was going to happen someday, I had to be
there to see it. During my whole life, all I've ever imagined for
Jono was to see him walk and run, which he was never able to do
during his entire life. I came to realize if that happens when Jono
is raised to eternal life with Jesus, and I miss out on it, it would be
the greatest tragedy of my life.

For me, all the suffering my family and I went through with Jono will be worth it if it means I get to see him walk or run someday.

That's why these words of Jesus give me so much hope.

That's why they encourage me to keep going when things get tough.

These words are both a warning and a source of encouragement. They are a warning to the people who are wealthy and powerful, but they encourage those of us who feel like we're the least and last. They're meant to encourage those of us who commit ourselves to following Jesus, and serving others in his name, which is anything but easy. These words are good news for the weak and broken, and for the people who feel like they're just barely making it.

If you ask me, that's great news, because that's how I feel most of the time.

If you feel the same way, then take heart and be encouraged, because now you know the hardship and suffering you go through in your life and service won't be in vain.

For those of us who follow Jesus by serving others, and putting their needs above our own, our reward will be great!

All Who Exalt Themselves Will Be Humbled

In Luke 14:7–11, Jesus is invited to the house of a Pharisee on the sabbath, and he takes advantage of the opportunity to tell a parable about a meal like the one they are sharing together. He tells everyone that when they go to a party, they should sit in the worst seat there. That way the person who invites them will see them, and call them up to a better seat.

Jesus says that guest will be honored in front of all the other guests, and then he finishes by saying these words: *"For all who exalt themselves will be humbled, and those who humble themselves will be exalted."* [66]

I love this paradox for the same reason I love the one just above. These words are both a warning and an encouragement. They warn the people who are proud and arrogant, but they encourage the people who humbly follow Jesus, and who humble themselves as they serve him. These words look to the future when God will establish his kingdom forever on the earth, and they tell us that only those who humble themselves now will be exalted for eternity later.

Likewise, those people who exalt themselves now won't be exalted later.

That means we can commit ourselves to humbly following and serving Jesus now by humbly serving others, and we can be assured that we will be repaid for whatever hardship and difficulty we encounter. In fact, even if we are killed in the process, these words assure us that the death of our bodies in this life doesn't mean eternal death or condemnation for us.

Dying, or being killed, as we serve Jesus is the ultimate form of humbling ourselves, so these words should encourage us to boldly follow Jesus into potentially dangerous situations.

In fact, this is now how I think of my younger brother Jono, and how I processed his death when he died in his sleep at the age of 21. Jono had lived as much as his broken body would let him.

There was nothing more he could do, and now I wait with joy and excitement when I think about how incredibly exalted he will be when he is exalted forever with Jesus. In fact, that's truly good news that gives me goosebumps and makes me cry every time I think about him.

Faith Like a Child

At one point, Jesus's disciples ask him who is the greatest in the kingdom of heaven. They were arguing about it and they want to know from their teacher: *which one of us is the greatest?* In other words: *which one of us is the best? Which one of us is number one?* Matthew's Gospel records Jesus's response to that question:

> He called a child, whom he put among them, and said, "Truly I tell you, unless you change and become like children, you will never enter the kingdom of heaven. Whoever becomes humble like this child is the greatest in the kingdom of heaven. Whoever welcomes one such child in my name welcomes me." [67]

Jesus calls a child so all his disciples can see exactly who he's talking about. Then he says they need to become like that child. But how can they do this since they're grown men? To what is Jesus referring when he says disciples need to become like children?

First: Jesus says his disciples need to humble themselves like a child, because adults often try to show everyone just how strong and powerful we are. Adults usually try to prove our value and worth to other people. But very small children don't really do this. They know they're weak and dependent on mommy and daddy, and they're reminded of this every time they want to eat, drink, or do anything that depends on adults helping them.

When Jesus talks about humbling ourselves in these verses, I think he is saying that he wants his disciples to recognize our weakness and dependence on him.

Without him, we are hopelessly lost and inadequate.

Second: I don't think Jesus is saying he wants us to return to the ignorance of small children. Small children are ignorant of reality because they haven't experienced much of it. They have no way of knowing about many things until they learn about them when they grow up. I don't think Jesus wants us to return to that kind of blind ignorance, even though it seems like far too many American Christians fall into that trap.

Trusting Jesus with our lives doesn't mean blindly trusting him or anything else, and Christians who fall into blind trust quickly fall into blind ignorance.

But there is nothing remotely godly or good about blind ignorance.

Instead, I think Jesus is calling us to trust him in the same way small children trust their parents.

We are to trust with an informed trust that recognizes our shortcomings and needs, just like small children do with their parents. Parents help small children learn and explore the real world, little by little. They teach them about what is right and wrong, and what is good and bad. They also encourage and support young children as they set out to discover the world, and I think this kind of trust is what Jesus wants his followers to have.

Jesus wants us to trust in him just like a small child trusts his or her parents.

The Beatitudes

Jesus begins his longest teaching in the New Testament, which is all about the kinds of actions and things he wants his followers to do, with these words about who is truly blessed or happy: [68]

Blessed are the poor in spirit, for theirs is the kingdom of heaven. Blessed are those who mourn, for they will be comforted. Blessed are the meek, for they will inherit the earth. Blessed are those who hunger and thirst for righteousness, for they will be filled. Blessed are the merciful, for they will receive mercy. Blessed are the pure in heart, for they will see God. Blessed are the peacemakers, for they will be called children of God. Blessed are those who are persecuted for righteousness' sake, for theirs is the kingdom of heaven. Blessed are you when people revile you and persecute you and utter all kinds of evil against you falsely on my account. Rejoice and be glad, for your reward is great in heaven, for in the same way they persecuted the prophets who were before you. [69]

I love these words because they flip over all the ways our world defines who is truly blessed and happy. Our world looks around and says the truly blessed and happy ones are the wealthy and powerful. They are the ones who live it up by throwing all kinds of expensive and extravagant parties and events.

They're the ones who seem to have just about everything.

These are the people who hunger and thirst for more and more of whatever they have.

They get revenge and pursue the road of violence and destruction.

They have crooked hearts and motives, which are acted out in their lives.

The Jews during the time of Jesus viewed the almighty Roman Empire in just this way.

The Jews despised the Romans, and viewed them as godless pagans who were so entrenched in their idolatry and sexual immorality that most Jews thought the only way to stop them was to destroy them. But for the Jews, that was the problem; they had been completely overtaken by the Romans, which meant they had no power or means whatsoever to stand up to Rome. After all, at that time, Rome was the greatest military and political force the world had ever seen.

But just as the Jews were getting swept away in their anger, bitterness, rage, and hatred of the Romans, Jesus called his Jewish followers to a completely different way of living and viewing the world, including the hated Romans. And from the perspective of eternity in God's kingdom, the poor in spirit, the meek, the merciful, the peacemakers, and those who are persecuted are the truly blessed and happy ones because they will receive their reward of eternity with God.

In fact, Jesus is the only person who can say something like this because only he knows exactly what our future reward will be. You and I, along with every other human being who has ever lived, simply don't know. That means we need to trust what he says and live our lives in light of these words.

I experienced this powerfully when I was in Bolivia for a month, doing ministry with a missions organization based out of Chile. [70] At one point, we were waiting for the pastor of the church we were working with to get to the church, and our whole team was sitting down on the front steps of the church.

I was the only one standing up, and I saw a man who was very drunk start to walk towards me from across the street. I was standing there with my hands tucked into the front pockets of the jacket I was wearing. We were staring at each other as he made his way towards me, while the rest of my team didn't even know the guy was coming.

They were all sitting and lying down on the steps of the church as the man approached me. Neither one of us said anything, but when he was about 7–10 feet away from me, he reached in his two back pockets with each hand, and pulled out two steak knives that both had blades about 6 inches long.

When I saw the knives, I immediately thought: *I could get ready to attack or fight this guy, but that would mean I would be fighting a man with two huge knives.*

I figured any fight or struggle would most likely end up with me dead or severely injured, so I wanted to avoid that at all costs.

At that point, I was overcome with a very strange sense of peace and absolute calm.

Now, I fully believe that peace came from the spirit of God, which I think he poured out on me to remain calm and collected.

I also knew that if I died right there on those church steps in Bolivia, as I was serving God, then that would be a great way to go. I knew I had humbled myself serving God, and would be exalted and rewarded in the future.

But, guess what?

I didn't die.

Everything happened so quickly that I didn't have time to think. I just reacted. Within a split second, the guy raised one knife up over the back of my right shoulder, and the other one out over my left ribs. Then he started the motion of slamming them down into my flesh, like he was going to stab me.

I just kept staring silently at his face.

Without moving a muscle.

But he didn't stab me.

He stopped just as the knives were about to touch my skin.

My hands were still tucked in the front pockets of my jacket.

I never took them out or moved at all.

I just stood there.

Staring at the guy.

Whose face was now about two inches away from mine.

Then he stopped moving briefly, and we stared silently at one another. After the brief period of stillness, he smirked at me with the smile of someone who was crazy, and walked away. He ran across the street and took off in a taxi that was parked over there.

During the whole interaction, we never said one word or even made one sound.

It was completely silent.

But God gave me a divine peace and assurance during the whole thing.

I tell you this so you see that, if we have the courage to follow him, often Jesus will lead us into dangerous and scary situations where death or real pain and suffering are possibilities. But he also assures us that if we suffer because of that, even if we suffer death, then we should be encouraged by the fact that we will spend eternity with him.

And that means we truly will be the blessed and happy ones.

Whoever Wants to Be First Must Be Last

There are a few places where Jesus says that whoever wants to be first must be the very last, and the servant of everyone else. [71] These words, once again, seem contradictory at first glance, but make much more sense when we take a closer look. At one point, Jesus's disciples are arguing over which one of them is the greatest, and when Jesus confronts them by asking about their argument, he responds by telling them these famous words: *"Whoever wants to be first must be last of all and servant of all."* [72]

Jesus's disciples assume that being great is all about receiving things like recognition, honor, glory, fame, gratitude, and appreciation. They see greatness in the same way as most people in our world, including even most confessed Christians. We normally define greatness by trying to outrank all the other people in our world, so we appear to be superior to them when we compare ourselves.

In fact, in this interaction, that's exactly what Jesus's own disciples were doing.

They were walking along a road.

And they were arguing about which one was the greatest.

Then, later, Jesus asks them about it and confronts their mistaken thinking.

According to Jesus's definition, his followers shouldn't look to the people the world defines as great. Instead we should look at the people who live their lives serving the least of their fellow human beings. That means followers of Jesus should stop looking to people like Bill Gates, Warren Buffett, or Steve Jobs when we think of greatness. Instead, we should look to people who were the last, and served the least among us.

I'm talking about people like Mother Theresa and Dr. Martin Luther King Jr.

For Christians and followers of Jesus, these kinds of people lived so sacrificially, and in-line with Jesus's definition of serving the least in our societies, that we should define greatness by the kinds of loving service they lived out. We should hold them up as the banner to shoot for, instead of praising people who go after things like power, money, fame, and influence.

Those things make someone great in the eyes of our world, but they don't make us great in the eyes of Jesus. And if we take our faith in Jesus even half-serious, then we should default to his definition.

A similar passage is when Jesus says his followers shouldn't lead like the rest of the world does, but rather they should lead by serving. Two of Jesus's followers ask him if they can have special seats of honor when he establishes his kingdom on the earth, and Jesus responds by telling them:

> *You know that among the Gentiles those whom they recognize as their rulers lord it over them, and their great ones are tyrants over them. But it is not so among you; but whoever wishes to become great among you must be your servant, and whoever wishes to be first among you must be slave of all. For the Son of Man came not to be served but to serve, and to give his life a ransom for many.* [73]

This request from two of Jesus's followers shows that they were highly interested in the same things most of us are: recognition, honor, fame, glory, and power. Unfortunately, these are the same kinds of things most Christians today still go after, mistakenly thinking these things will make them great.

But Jesus will not have any of this.

He says the leaders of the gentiles—such as the Romans—lord their power, authority, prestige, and position over their people. But he says his followers are not to follow the ways of the gentiles.

Instead, followers of Jesus are to serve and be the servant of everyone.

Why is this such a big deal to Jesus?

Because of what he says in the final verse: he didn't come to be served, but to serve and give his life to set people free. And if we dare to call ourselves disciples or followers of Jesus—which is the only term he ever uses to describe his people—then we must actually follow his words and actions.

We should do what he did.

After all, that's the only way we can follow him.

We need to learn from his example and serve the least around us if we want to be truly great.

Otherwise, we're just following the misguided notions of greatness that Jesus was correcting in his own disciples when they started arguing over which one was the greatest.

God Hides from the Intelligent and Reveals to the Simple

At one point, Jesus says that his Father hides things from those who are wise and intelligent, and reveals them to people who are not:

> At that same hour Jesus rejoiced in the Holy Spirit and said, "I thank you, Father, Lord of heaven and earth, because you have hidden these things from the wise and the intelligent and have revealed them to infants; yes, Father, for such was your gracious will. [74]

Why does God like to hide things from the intelligent and wise people?

Probably because those kinds of people tend to trust and rely so much on their own intelligence, logic, reason, and capabilities that they almost never trust or rely on God. These kinds of people tend to be arrogant and prideful because they know how capable they are of handling most things they encounter in life. That means these kinds of people have been trained by their own intelligence to trust in themselves instead of trusting God.

Being intelligent often trains people to be prideful and arrogant, but these are the exact opposite qualities God wants his people to have.

God wants us to be humble and recognize our dependence.

God wants us to trust in him instead of always trusting in ourselves.

He wants us to humble ourselves and recognize our limitations and faults.

But the wise and intelligent people have a hard time doing that.

Jesus thanks his father and says he has revealed himself to infants, meaning to the kinds of people who are weak, meek, vulnerable, and humble like infants all are. According to Jesus, these humble people are the kinds of people God reveals himself to. That means we should all strive to develop humility and recognize our need for God, even if we are the smartest person around.

This doesn't mean we need to be dumb or ignorant to follow Jesus.

When Jesus says this, he's showing us the kinds of qualities we need to pursue if we want God to reveal himself to us. God doesn't like people who are prideful or arrogant, so he rarely reveals himself to those kinds of people. That means we should avoid those qualities if we want him to reveal himself to us, because he prefers people who resemble infants in their dependence and humility.

That means we should pursue those child-like qualities if we want God to reveal himself to us.

Sick People Need Doctors

Jesus called a man named Levi, who was a tax-collector, to follow him; and Levi did. Then Levi threw a party for Jesus at his house, and this happened:

> *Levi gave a great banquet for him in his house; and there was a large crowd of tax collectors and others sitting at the table with them. The Pharisees and their scribes were complaining to his disciples, saying, "Why do you eat and drink with tax collectors and sinners?" Jesus answered, "Those who are well have no need of a physician, but those who are sick; I have come to call not the righteous but sinners to repentance."* [75]

There was a large crowd of tax collectors and notorious sinners at the party, so much so that at one point, the Jewish religious leaders there complain to Jesus's disciples that they all eat and drink with tax collectors and sinners. Apparently, what Jesus and his disciples were doing was just too scandalous for the very proper Jewish religious leaders, who were outraged that Jesus would share tables, food, community, and life with such a rag-tag group of hopeless sinners.

Jesus responds by saying the people who need doctors are the sick, not those who are well.

Then he says he came to call sinners—not the righteous—to repentance.

Jesus means that, just like a doctor must spend his or her time tending to the sick, so, too, must Jesus tend to the people who are spiritually, socially, or even physically sick. And he can only do that by spending time with those kinds of people.

I love these words because I, too, was spiritually sick and needed Jesus to make me well.

And do you know what?

He did.

And he wants to do the same with you, if you will let him.

9

WEALTH

Jesus speaks a ton about wealth and money, often alienating the powerful. Money isn't inherently bad, but it is extremely dangerous. In a way that few things do, it has astonishing power to corrupt our ethics, hearts, minds, lives, faith, families, and discipleship.

Camels Going Through Eyes of Needles

At one point, Jesus is talking about wealth and says to his disciples:

> "How hard it will be for those who have wealth to enter the kingdom of God!" And the disciples were perplexed at these words. But Jesus said to them again, "Children, how hard it is to enter the kingdom of God! It is easier for a camel to go through the eye of a needle than for someone who is rich to enter the kingdom of God." They were greatly astounded and said to one another, "Then who can be saved?" Jesus

looked at them and said, "For mortals it is impossible, but not for God;
for God all things are possible." [76]

These words are fascinating for a couple reasons. First: Jesus says it's harder for a camel, which is a massive animal, to go through the eye of a needle, which is incredibly tiny, then it is for a rich person to enter the kingdom of God. Even though Jesus is using hyperbole, which is like exaggeration, to make his point, he still makes his point: it will be very hard for rich people to enter into the kingdom of God.

In fact, it will be so hard that when his disciples ask who can be saved, he doesn't tell them not to worry.

He says it's impossible for human beings, but not so for God.

Jesus seems to be saying that even though many rich people will not enter the kingdom of God, not all of them will share that fate. After all, for God, all things are possible. This should be a grave warning for all the wealthy people reading this: your wealth might prohibit you from entering into God's kingdom when you die.

Second: We live in the wealthiest nation the world has ever seen, even though many Christians are clueless about how the rest of the world actually lives. [77]

During my 6.5 years in Latin America, I got a first-hand taste of what it's like to live in developing 3rd world nations, and it's like living in a whole different world. I was always so stricken by the fact that I could get on a plane and end up back home in California on any given day—it often seemed to me like I was living not just in a different place, but in a different time.

Everything in developing countries is delayed compared to what we have in the USA. Nothing works as well as what we have here. It seemed like I was living 50–100 years ago. Now, I know there are wealthy Latin Americans and poor Americans, but, generally speaking, Latin Americans are so much poorer than Americans that it boggles the mind.

My point is that if you are an American reading this, you might not think you are rich; but the vast majority of the rest of the world only dreams, in their wildest fantasies, of living the life you live.

For example: do you have a car?

Do you have a refrigerator?

Do you have a freezer?

Do you have a TV?

Do you have a microwave?

Do you have your own bed?

Do you have a computer?

If you said yes to any of these, then you should know that you're so rich that the vast majority of people in the world dream of your life, because they will never be able to attain those simple items. The truth is, we may not feel rich, but we are; and, once again, certainly not every American is rich, but the vast majority are when we compare ourselves to the rest of the world.

Did you know half the world lives on less than a few dollars per day?

I hope that now you're able to see how rich you are.

If that's true, then how can we respond?

By being generous with our money and giving it to those in need.

Give it away to organizations and churches.

Give it away to people in need at shelters or rehabilitation houses, and to the people who serve others.

Following Jesus means he is the lord and master of our life, and that means money and wealth can't be. Too many American Christians bow down to the god of money, and therefore commit idolatry towards Jesus. We are supposed to be faithful to his teachings and words before anyone, or anything, else. If not, then, like Jesus says here, we might not enter into the kingdom of God.

Much Is Expected from Those Who Have Much

Jesus tells a parable about being faithful with what we've been given, and then finishes with these words:

> *From everyone to whom much has been given, much will be required; and from the one to whom much has been entrusted, even more will be demanded.* [78]

These words tell us that, to the person who has been given much, much will be required when we die; but to the person who has been trusted with much, even more will be required. What do these verses mean? They mean that if we have been given many resources like food or money, then, in order to enter into God's kingdom, much will be required of us when we go to judgment.

These verses show us there are no free passes into eternal life. For every person who has been given much, they will be held accountable to give that much more to assure their place in the kingdom of God. To the person who has been given less, less will be required.

These verses should come as a warning to those wealthy Americans who think they can oppress people and live however they want just because they think they're saved from saying a prayer once. Maybe they are, but these verses, and others like them, seem to paint a very different picture of judgment; and I wouldn't count your chickens before they hatch.

These are strangely fascinating words, but they tell us that we will be held accountable to the amount of resources and things God gives us. These verses should make us think twice about sitting back on our massive bank accounts and retirement accounts. Instead, we should choose to invest those things in ways that help us follow and serve Jesus faithfully wherever we are.

Impossible to Serve Both God and Money

Jesus said this about serving God and money:

> *No slave can serve two masters; for a slave will either hate the one and love the other, or be devoted to the one and despise the other. You cannot serve God and wealth.* [79]

These words are especially true for us, since we live in the wealthiest country the world has ever seen. We are a people who have devoted ourselves to doing the very thing Jesus says we can't do: serving God and money. [80] Like no other country on earth, we have bowed down to the mighty power that money has given us.

We have made our lives and homes in its shade.

But, according to Jesus, this is completely inappropriate for followers of Jesus.

During my years living in the impoverished developing 3rd world nations of Latin America, and experiencing life as close to being a Latin-American as I could, I would argue that the American church has bowed down so low to the idols of money and wealth that we can barely even see Jesus.

We constantly compromise on his crystal-clear teachings and ethics if it means we can earn more money. We cut ethical corners and betray our primary allegiance to Jesus just to earn extra money. This is exactly what so many American Christians do, but, according to Jesus, we can't do that.

We can't serve both God and money, because the money will eventually call us to compromise on the calling God has given us.

We need to let Jesus be the rightful lord and master of our lives, and make everything else in our lives bow to him. That's the only way we'll be able to maintain the calling he gives to everyone who dares to follow him.

10

LOVE FOR ENEMIES

Over and over again, Jesus calls his followers to reject all violence and war. In fact, as we will see below, he even makes a pre-condition by saying that if we are not loving and praying for our enemies, then we are not the children of God we think we are. Contrary to our cultural tendencies, Jesus calls us to respond to evil with love and forgiveness, and to never retaliate with violence or aggression. We desperately need to adopt the same radical, self-sacrificial love of Jesus.

Loving and Praying for Enemies

I have written extensively about Jesus's commands for us to love our enemies in my other books, so I won't say too much about that here. [81] But I did want to give you the text and say a few things:

You have heard that it was said, "You shall love your neighbor and hate your enemy." But I say to you, Love your enemies and pray for those who persecute you, so that you may be children of your Father in heaven; for he makes his sun rise on the evil and on the good, and sends rain on the righteous and on the unrighteous. For if you love those who love you, what reward do you have? Do not even the tax collectors do the same? And if you greet only your brothers and sister what more are you doing than others? Do not even the Gentiles do the same? Be perfect, therefore, as your heavenly Father is perfect. [82]

When Jesus talks about loving neighbors, he's referring to commands from the Jewish scriptures, which is what Christians call the Old Testament. But nowhere does it say they were supposed to hate their enemies. At the time of Jesus, that was the common Jewish interpretation of the verses about loving neighbors.

For Jews, loving neighbors meant loving their fellow Jews who happened to live close to them, but they notoriously hated and despised all the other nations of antiquity. They despised the people from those nations, too. In the time of Jesus, the enemies took the form of the Roman Empire, which Jews hated more than anything else.

They also hated the Romans who made up the Roman Empire, and longed for the day when they might destroy it.

Because of this, faithful Jews thought they were supposed to love and serve God, love and serve their Jewish neighbors, and then hate all the non-Jews. And this is why Jesus starts by saying that's exactly what the Jewish people have heard up until then.

But, for followers of Jesus, that goes against everything he stood for.

For followers of Jesus, the game has changed forever.

Jesus tells his Jewish followers that they should love and pray for not only their fellow Jewish neighbors, but also for their enemies *so that* they may be children of their heavenly Father. The words *so that* imply that they can't be children of God unless they love their enemies and pray for those who persecute them, just like I eat *so that* I'm no longer hungry.

Now, these words apply to every single Christian and follower of Jesus.

That means they apply to you.

This is staggering.

Jesus says our identity as members of his family, what Christians call being saved, can't be attained unless we first love our enemies and pray for those who persecute us.

Why is this a big deal for Jesus?

Because, according to him, that's how God is.

God lets the rain and sun fall on the good and bad people alike. In the same way, we are to model the all-embracing love of God by embracing everyone we come across, including even our enemies and the people we hate.

Then Jesus drives the point even further by saying that if we love only those who love us, or if we greet and take into account only those people who greet us and take us into account, then we are no better than tax collectors and gentiles. As you may remember, *gentiles* was a term Jews used to refer to non-Jewish people, and tax-collectors were possibly the only group Jews hated more than the non-Jewish gentiles. Tax collectors were Jews who betrayed their own flesh and blood by working for the Romans, collecting taxes from the Jews, which they gave to the Romans.

Most Jews regarded tax collectors as less-than-human, but Jesus says that if we love only the people who love us, then we aren't doing anything that the gentiles and tax collectors aren't already doing. After all, tax collectors, gentiles, and even the worst people on earth all love and protect their own family and friends.

They all love and protect the people who love and protect them.

In fact, this is even true of Adolph Hitler, Charles Manson, and the worst people you can think of.

They all love and care for the people who love and care for them. If that's all we do as Christians and followers of Jesus, then, as Jesus says, we will not get any reward.

Unfortunately, the vast majority of American Christians today fall into the exact cycle that Jesus says we can't fall into if we want to be children of God. Most American Christians love and care for their family, friends, and neighbors in ways that lead them to support and endorse violence and warfare against anyone who threatens their family, friends, or neighbors.

This also means that when Christians fight in the military, or support those who do, they are falling into the exact same trap Jesus warned the Jews of his day not to fall into. This is the same trap that led all the Christians in Europe, led by the Catholic Church, to launch holy wars against Muslims in Jerusalem during the middle ages. Those wars, which we now call the crusades, were among the most bloody and horrific wars in human history. [83]

What do we see in all these examples?

We see Christians killing their enemies, in the name of Jesus and to the glory of God.

We see Christians killing other Christians if they happen to be from a different country.

We also see Christians killing Christians who might threaten or disagree with them.

But all of these people have fallen away from the teachings of Jesus.

None of the people who claim the name of Jesus but share those views are actually following the teachings of Jesus.

Every single one has gone astray.

That means you, too, if you support and endorse this violence or warfare.

Jesus calls his followers to love and pray even for our enemies, which could be ISIS, the gang in your neighborhood, Muslims, the LGBTQ community, atheists, conservatives, liberals, and anyone else you may consider an enemy. This is why it's completely inappropriate for any Christians to partake in violence or war, unless you want to deny or contradict the crystal-clear teachings of Jesus on that issue. [84]

If that's how you want to live, then go ahead.

But know that you have severed yourself completely from the teachings and person of Jesus.

You can call yourself whatever you want.

But Jesus sees what you do.

He knows the truth.

And none of us can hide from that.

If you're a Christian who supports violence, you need to know that, according to these words of Jesus, you're not the child of God you think you are.

I didn't say that.

Jesus did.

As for the rest of us, I hope and pray we have the courage and strength to choose the same self-sacrificial, non-violent enemy-love as Jesus.

Are you with me?

An Eye for an Eye

At one point in the middle of the Sermon on the Mount, Jesus says this:

> You have heard that it was said, "An eye for an eye and a tooth for a tooth." But I say to you, Do not resist an evildoer. But if anyone strikes you on the right cheek, turn the other also; and if anyone wants to sue you and take your coat, give your cloak as well; and if anyone forces you to go one mile, go also the second mile. Give to everyone who begs from you, and do not refuse anyone who wants to borrow from you. [85]

Why is this so radical? Because our whole world lives on the eye-for-eye, tit-for-tat ethic that Jesus condemns with these words. According to Jesus, his followers should not seek revenge or vengeance on anyone. But before we go any further, I want to clear up a misunderstanding about the Greek word translated as "*resist*" when it talks about resisting an evildoer.

That word doesn't mean we should resist by just lying down like doormats so everyone runs all over us. It actually carries the meaning of resisting by doing the same evil thing back to the person who did it to you first. Jesus is calling his followers not to resist an evildoer if it means we commit the same evil, or something worse, when we respond to the person who did the first evil thing to us.

But if that's true, then why do so many American Christians respond to insults and attacks by insulting and attacking right back?

Why do so many American Christians see no problem with committing attacks of violence, aggression, and destruction against people they happen to view as enemies, targets, or problems? Don't they realize they aren't following the teachings of Jesus when they do that? Don't they recognize they are no longer following Jesus when they do that?

I hope you can see how revolutionary Jesus's words are.

He calls us to live out an absolutely revolutionary form of non-violent love, grace, forgiveness, and redemption.

He calls us to respond to violence with non-violence.

He calls us to refuse to get caught up in the endless cycles of eye-for-eye retaliation and revenge. Tragically, most self-proclaiming

Christians either deny or ignore these words altogether. That might be the only way they can sleep at night because, if they took their faith and commitment to Jesus half as seriously as they say they do, they would drop their violent agendas and submit to the self-sacrificial, non-violent enemy-love and agenda of Jesus.

After all, that's what Jesus expected all his followers to do when he said these words.

He expected every single one of them to adopt these ethics for their lives.

And these words still call everyone who dares to come to Jesus or claim his name. It doesn't matter what we say about ourselves, or what we call ourselves; if we're not living out this ethic, then we're not following Jesus, which means we're not the Christians we think we are.

Put Your Sword Back

When the Jewish religious leaders come to arrest Jesus, Peter takes out his sword and cuts off the ear of the servant of the high priest. When he does this, Jesus doesn't say: *way to go, Peter! Everyone attack!* Instead, he rebukes Peter's violent action with these words: "*Put your sword back into its place; for all who take the sword will perish by the sword.*" [86]

With these words, Jesus once again rules out violence for his followers. He states the obvious: everyone who lives by the sword will die by it.

Today, we could substitute swords for all kinds of things:

Guns.

Bombs.

Tanks.

Grenades.

Fighter jets.

Nuclear bombs.

It doesn't matter what we put in there.

It's inappropriate for any follower of Jesus to use those things against anyone.

But if that's true, then why do so many American Christians seem perfectly fine doing that very thing? That's a question I don't have the answer to, but it's one of the reasons I started writing books. I wanted to call those Christians out for their hypocrisy and failure to follow the man they claim to follow.

Because, if they were authentic followers of Jesus, then they would drop their violent and hidden agendas. They would recognize that every ethical teaching of Jesus and the New Testament calls them to act and react with the same self-sacrificial, non-violent, enemy-love of Jesus.

We are called to live out something radically different than the rest of the non-Christian world. When non-Christians go to war to fight in the name of their god, they are doing the same thing human beings have done since the dawn of history. All the Christians who attack, destroy, and kill in the name of Jesus are simply using the name of their God to fall into the vicious and endless cycles of retaliatory violence and vengeance that the world already operates by.

The same is true for every Christian soldier who goes to war to kill the same enemies Jesus calls us to love and pray for.

This is why Jesus calls his followers, again and again, to refuse violence against anyone.

It's impossible to serve the purposes of Jesus by attacking and killing other human beings, because, according to the New Testament, human beings aren't our enemies.

Satan is our enemy.

And we can't attack or destroy Satan by attacking or destroying human beings. [87]

Jesus calls us to something completely different.

Jesus calls us to live out the same radical non-violent, self-sacrificial enemy-love that he lived and demonstrated.

Folks, if you're looking for a revolution, then you found it.

Father Forgive Them, for They Know Not What They Do

Jesus has just been crucified and yet he stops to pray for his enemies, who are the very people who are executing him! Here are his words: *"Father, forgive them; for they do not know what they are doing."* [88] To me, these are some of the most radical, shocking, surprising, beautiful, and loving words anywhere in all of scripture!

This is Jesus putting into practice his command to love and pray for our enemies. Any follower of Jesus who thinks those words don't apply to them has completely misunderstood his message. This loving prayer on behalf of his executioners reveals the loving heart Jesus has towards the world that largely has rejected him.

It reveals a broken heart.

It reveals a love so strong, it longs to gather the children of Jerusalem to protect them, but they are unwilling. [89]

They don't want to be gathered together.

So they reject the only one who can bring them true peace.

They reject the only one who can save them.

It's like a Greek tragedy, but worse, because it's real life.

These people executed the person God sent to save them.

They executed the one God sent to teach them the road of peace and love.

They executed the one God sent to heal and restore them.

They executed, insulted, and ridiculed the one God sent as their rightful king.

And how did Jesus respond?

He didn't attack them.

He didn't try to get even.

He prayed for them.

And then he gave his life for them.

That, friends, is love.

That's my hero.

CONCLUSION: HOW SHOULD WE RESPOND?

As we have seen, Jesus was about as far from boring and ordinary as anyone can be. As I said at the beginning of this book, people don't get executed like he was for being boring, nice, or kind. They don't get executed for simply going along with the status quo, either. That's why I said there is no way Jesus is actually like the characters of Mr. Rogers or Santa Claus that I think lots of us identify him with.

Jesus was the ultimate revolutionary of human history. He challenged just about everything: He challenged and fought against social injustices, religious injustices, religiosity, religious pride and arrogance, religious ignorance, personal bondage, economic bondage, social bondage, and a host of other things. These are the kinds of actions that get people executed.

Jesus turned over the values that our cultures and societies are all built on. He taught with his words and deeds about a different way to live, and he calls each of his followers to follow him by doing what he does. He calls us out of the ignorance that the rest of the world operates under, and he calls us to follow him and his ways.

As I have said in this book, this isn't easy or comfortable, but Jesus doesn't seem to care much about that. He still did these things, and he still calls us to follow him and follow his example.

Learning from Jesus how to put the needs of others before our own isn't easy.

Learning how to refuse to retaliate and get revenge isn't easy.

Learning how to refuse to use, or respond with, violence isn't easy.

Learning how to forgive without end, and seek reconciliation, isn't easy.

Learning how to love and pray for our enemies isn't easy.

Learning how to make peace isn't easy.

Learning how to humble ourselves and serve people isn't easy.

Learning how to put to death the things we used to do isn't easy.

Learning how to depend on God's power and strength, instead of our own, isn't easy.

Learning how to follow God's will for our lives, instead of what everyone else tells us, isn't easy.

Learning how to depend on God, instead of being independent, isn't easy.

I could keep going, but I think you get my point; none of these things are easy, but Jesus did them and calls us to do them, too, if we take our faith in him seriously.

This is no game.

This is serious business that demands our full attention.

No half-measures will do.

We're either in, or we're out.

Jesus has left us no other option.

He didn't intend to.

So how will you respond?

Will you start to view Jesus as the ultimate revolutionary of human history that he is, or will you keep thinking of him like a fantasy figure not unlike Mr. Rogers, Santa Claus, Big Bird, or the Cookie Monster? We can't possibly discover and appreciate the real historical Jesus until we drop our fantasy-like assumptions and preconceived notions about him. As long as we continue in those inaccurate views, we'll never be able to take Jesus seriously.

And if we can't take the person of Jesus as seriously as we do every other human being of history, then we'll never be able to come to terms with just how radical, subversive, scandalous, and countercultural his teachings and life were. We'll also never be able to come to terms with how radical the calling he gives us is, since we won't let him be the actual historical person he was and is.

When we let him be the revolutionary he was, then we'll start to discover just how radical he still is.

We'll realize and appreciate just how brilliant, insightful, discerning, loving, courageous, and strong he is, and use him as the example we should shoot for in our lives. Suddenly, as we set out to follow him and his ways, the same radical love, humility, strength, power, courage, bravery, and discernment he demonstrated will start to show up in our lives.

This is how we participate in the revolution Jesus started.

This is how we participate in God's great story of redeeming all of creation.

This is how we pass the baton to the next generation, realizing that we are the most recent among the people of God, but that we sit atop thousands of years of human history during which God has been working to bring his kingdom story to its final culmination.

This is how we play our part in the cosmic drama that God is working out in history.

This is how we become revolutionaries of self-sacrificial love.

This is how we become revolutionaries of, and with, Jesus.

This is how we participate with God in what he is doing in the world.

This is how we tell everyone the good news of Jesus.

This is how we take Jesus as seriously as he demands to be taken.

If that doesn't get you excited and pumped up, then I don't know what will.

ACKNOWLEDGMENTS

Thanks to everyone who helped me discover just how radical the real Jesus is: Mike Erre, the fellas (you know who you are), Fuller Seminary, Glen Stassen, C. S. Lewis, N. T. Wright, Dr. Martin Luther King Jr., Ray Anderson, and Greg Boyd.

Thanks to my wife Melanie, and my entire family, for all your love and support.

Thanks to the community of Redemption Church for all the love and support you have given Melanie and me in our first 2.5 years of marriage.

Thanks again to Andrew Kroeger at Barton Hill Books. Your changes made this book so much better than it was originally. No one else knows what the original manuscript was like, but your changes improved and focused it so much that it's almost a whole different book. Thanks so much for all your hard work! I don't know how you do what you do, but here's to the next one!

NOTES

1. Matthew 4:17; Luke 4:43; John 3:3.
2. Mark 1:15. NRSV.
3. The vast majority of theologians now recognize the kingdom of God is the central theme of not only the New Testament, but the entire Bible.
4. I make this point many times in my book, Who Would Jesus Bomb? Exposing the Truth About American Violence And Warfare.
5. Luke 4:16–21. NRSV.
6. Matthew 7:15–27. NRSV.
7. John 6:35–38. See also John 6:41, 48, 51.
8. See Exodus 16.
9. John 8:12. NRSV.
10. Matthew 5:14. NRSV.
11. John 10:7–18. NRSV.
12. John 10:30, 38. NRSV.
13. Matthew 12:22–28.
14. For people interested in amazing books that argue in

favor of the historical Jesus, you must read: Letters from a Skeptic by Greg Boyd; The Case for Christ and The Case for the Real Jesus by Lee Strobel; The Case for the Resurrection of Jesus by Gary Habermas and Michael Licona; Jesus Under Fire by Michael Wilkins and J.P. Moreland; The Gospel Code by Ben Witherington III; Can We Trust The Gospels? by Mark Roberts; The Historical Reliability of the Gospels by Craig Blomberg; The New Testament and the People of God, Jesus and the Victory of God, The Resurrection of the Son of God, Simply Jesus, How God Became King all by N.T. Wright; The Jesus I Never Knew by Phillip Yancey. For more general apologetics you must read: Is God To Blame? by Greg Boyd, Mere Christianity by C.S. Lewis, What's So Great About Christianity by Dinesh D'Souza, The Language of God by Francis Collins, The Case for a Creator and The Case for Faith by Lee Strobel, Dawkins' God and The Dawkins Delusion? by Alister McGrath.

15. John 11:25–26. NRSV.

16. For the best treatment of the resurrection, you must read The Resurrection of the Son of God and Surprised By Hope: Rethinking Heaven, the Resurrection, and the Mission of the Church by N.T. Wright, who is the world's leading New Testament scholar.

17. Read 1 Corinthians 15 for the most detailed explanation of the resurrection and our resurrection bodies in scripture; and read The Resurrection of the Son of God and Surprised By Hope: Rethinking Heaven, the Resurrection, and the Mission of the Church by N.T. Wright.

18. See 1 Corinthians 15; Revelation 21:1–4, 22–27.

19. John 14:6–7. NRSV.

20. While this is true, C.S. Lewis does a brilliant job in "The Last Battle" of the Chronicles of Narnia showing how this is true while also showing how the way to Jesus is probably much more broad and open than most of us realize. He shows people coming to Aslan for judgment, who is the Christ-figure of the story; and I think the way Aslan deals with them must be close to how God deals with people when they come to him. I can't recommend that book enough for anyone who is interested in how God will judge Christians and non-Christians.

21. John 15:1–8. NRSV.

22. This is the main theme of my book, Fully Human: Why The Humanity of Jesus Changes Everything.

23. Matthew 24:36. NRSV.

24. Matthew 24:37–44. NRSV.

25. See Matthew 25:31–46.

26. Matthew 26:37–42. NRSV.

27. For more on this, read my book, Fully Human: Why the Humanity of Jesus Changes Everything.

28. I actually have pretty good ideas why, but I'll spare you that for now since that's not what this book is about. Maybe I'll get into that more in a future book.

29. Mark 15:33–34. NRSV.

30. Hebrews 2:14–18.

31. I deal with this extensively in part 2 of my book, Fully Human: Why The Humanity Of Jesus Changes Everything.

32. See more about this in my book, Fully Human: Why the Humanity of Jesus Changes Everything.

33. Matthew 21:31–32. NRSV.

34. Matthew 5:17.

35. For more on this, read the amazing book: Pagan Christianity? Exploring the Roots of Our Christian Practices by Frank Viola and George Barna.

36. Matthew 7:12. NRSV.

37. Mark 12:28–34. NRSV.

38. Deuteronomy 6:4–5.

39. Matthew 5:43–48.

40. John 13:34–35. See also John 14:21, 23–24; 15:10–13, 17.

41. For more on this, you must read Myth of Christian Nation by Greg Boyd, and my books, Who Would Jesus Bomb? Exposing The Truth About Christian Violence and Warfare, and Hateful Morons? How We Can Save American Christianity From Itself.

42. For more on this you must read The Spanish Inquisition: A Historical Revision by Henry Kamen, and A History Of Christianity Volume I: Beginnings To 1500 by Kenneth Scott Latourette.

43. Greg Boyd, Myth of a Christian Nation. p. 79.

44. I develop this more in my book, Who Would Jesus Bomb? Exposing The Truth About Christian Violence And Warfare.

45. There have always been non-violent Christians and groups within Christianity, but they are a tiny minority surrounded by a sea of violent Christians.

46. Matthew 7:1–5. NRSV.

47. Matthew 7:24–27. NRSV.

48. Jesus makes this point in Matthew 5:43–48.

49. John 20:21–22. NRSV.

50. John 14:12. NRSV.

51. John 21:15–19. NRSV.

52. Matthew 28:18–20. NRSV.

53. Matthew 7:13–14. NRSV.

54. Mark 8:34–36. NRSV. See also Matthew 16:24–26.

55. Mark 10:29–30. NRSV.

56. Luke 14:26. NRSV.

57. John 19:26–27.

58. Luke 21:17. NRSV.

59. Luke 23:34.

60. Matthew 5:43–48.

61. Matthew 5:38–42.

62. Matthew 6:12, 14–15; 18:21–22.

63. Matthew 7:24–27. I also develop this theme more in my book, Who Would Jesus Bomb? Exposing the Truth About Christian Violence and Warfare.

64. The four Gospels are the first four books in the New Testament: Matthew, Mark, Luke, & John. They record the life and ministry of Jesus.

65. Matthew 20:16.

66. Luke 14:11. NRSV. We see this again in Luke 18:9–14 & Matthew 23:12.

67. Matthew 18:2–5. NRSV.

68. The Greek word translated as blessed here literally means happy.

69. Matthew 5:3–12. NRSV.

70. I lived in Latin American for 6.5 years, doing missions and ministry for 5 of those.

71. Mark 9:33–35. See also Mark 10:42–45; Matthew 20:25–28.

72. Mark 9:35. NRSV.

73. Mark 10:42–45. NRSV.

74. Luke 10:21. NRSV.

75. Luke 5:29–32. NRSV.

76. Mark 10:23–27. NRSV.

77. For more on this you must read Rich Christians In An Age of Hunger, by Ronald Sider; and The Hole In Our Gospel, by Richard Stearns.

78. Luke 12:48. NRSV.

79. Luke 16:13. NRSV.

80. For more on this you must read Rich Christians In An Age of Hunger, by Ron Sider & The Hole In Our Gospel, by Richard Stearns.

81. Read my previous books, Hateful Morons? How We Can Save American Christianity From Itself and Who Would Jesus Bomb? Exposing The Truth About Christian Violence And Warfare.

82. Matthew 5:43–48. NRSV. See also Luke 6:27–36.

83. For more on this you must read God's War: A New History of the Crusades by Christopher Tyerman.

84. Once again, you must read my previous books, Hateful Morons? How We Can Save American Christianity From Itself and Who Would Jesus Bomb? Exposing the Truth About Christian Violence and Warfare.

85. Matthew 5:38–42. NRSV.

86. Matthew 26:52. NRSV.

87. I write extensively about this in my book, Who Would Jesus Bomb? Exposing the Truth About Christian Violence and Warfare.

88. Luke 23:34. NRSV.

89. Matthew 23:37.

ABOUT THE AUTHOR

I grew up in a Christian family but turned my back on God when I was 11 or 12. Shortly after, I got into partying and lived like that until coming to faith at 22.

My younger brother Jonathan was severely mentally and physically disabled. Jono could never say one word, take one step, sit, stand, walk, crawl, feed himself, roll over, or do anything for himself. After years of caring for Jono, we had to put him in a home where he lived until he died at 21.

I turned away from God, partly because of unanswered prayers for Jono, but God also used Jono to bring me back to him. My dad's words at Jono's funeral sum up our feelings: "I would never wish for someone like Jono even for my worst enemy, but I would never let anyone take away the experience of having him." We rarely talk about Jono because, when we do, we cry. He is the lens I see through. He shaped all my views about God, faith, suffering, pain, sorrow, joy, and meaning. He's also my reminder that, one day, all things will be made new.

After coming to faith in college, I devoted myself to reaching the skaters, surfers, and partiers I grew up around. Eventually I lived in Latin America for 6.5 years, and helped plant a church dedicated to reaching Chile's skaters, surfers, and young people. Since returning from Chile in 2014, I married Melanie, which was the best decision I ever made.

To find out more about me, please visit www.greghaugh.com.

THANKS FOR READING!

If this book has been helpful to you, a quick, honest review (which you can do on Amazon in less than a minute) will help more people discover this book. I'd love to hear your stories of how it has impacted you and your feedback will help me improve my future books.

WANT TO STAY UP-TO-DATE WITH MY NEW BOOKS?

Join my newsletter for great articles and behind-the-scenes looks at upcoming books. You'll also get instant access to my e-book *Bumper Sticker Theology*, where I share the faith lessons we can all learn from bumper stickers. It's a good one! To join, please visit www.greghaugh.com/join.

Made in the USA
Las Vegas, NV
10 September 2022

55060238R00094